P9-DNS-323

The Coastal Navigator's Notebook

Compiled and edited by Tony Gibbs

International Marine Publishing Company
Camden, Maine

By the same author
Practical Sailing
Pilot's Work Book/Pilot's Log Book
Powerboating
Sailing: A First Book
Backpacking
Navigation
Advanced Sailing
The Coastal Cruiser
Rough Log

Typeset by Journal Publications, Camden, Maine
Printed by The Alpine Press, Stoughton, Massachusetts

Published by International Marine Publishing Company
21 Elm Street, Camden, Maine 04843
(207) 236-4342

Library of Congress Cataloging in Publication Data

Gibbs, Tony, 1935-
  The Coastal Navigator's Notebook.

  Revision of: Pilot's work book.

  1. Coastwise navigation. 2. Navigation 3. Seamanship
    I. Pilot's work book. II. Title.
VK559.G5 1982   623.89′2   81-83864
ISBN 0-87742-149-8   AACR2

The tables on page 22 are from *Weather for the Mariner,* by Captain William J. Kotsch, USN. © 1970 by the United States Naval Institute. Reprinted with permission.

For Elaine and Bill and Eric

CONTENTS

NAVIGATOR'S DATA

(Tables to be completed by the navigator)

REFERENCE TABLES

PREFACE

The original version of this book, entitled **Pilot's Work Book,** and its companion, the **Pilot's Log Book,** were assembled a decade ago for the skipper/navigator who enjoys, or would like to enjoy, the process of piloting his vessel, as opposed to just aiming her at a succession of buoys.

The skills of coastal navigation are and ought to be a source of great satisfaction, as much so as a smoothly executed docking maneuver or a lightning spinnaker hoist. As with any undertaking, in order to realize the full potential of navigational instruments, as well as the talents of the navigator himself, practice is essential. This book was conceived to provide the reasonably proficient pilot with the convenient tables, shortcuts, and memory hints to make his practice more enjoyable and his execution more successful.

Since the original version of this book appeared, the hand calculator has become a major factor in all forms of navigation, and this has necessitated some revision, as has the normal practice of making the navigator responsible for communications as well. In short, it seemed like a good time to overhaul the book, and **The Coastal Navigator's Notebook** is the result. I hope that this revised and expanded work will be useful and enjoyable for a whole new generation of coastwise navigators.

Tony Gibbs

1/ WEATHER

Although the weather information required by the coastal pilot is not very complex, he does need accurate foreknowledge of conditions during the coming day (and possibly night), as well as a reasonably good idea of what's likely to be in store for the next two or three days. Weather forecasting is a continuing process that requires regular practice if new or existent trends are to be perceived. The pilot's weather observations should, therefore, begin substantially before he embarks — the night before a weekend trip, several days in advance of a longer voyage.

The pilot should have access to a list of radio stations along his route that give comprehensive, marine forecasts at convenient times. Some commercial stations are excellent; so are the National Weather Service VHF/FM stations listed in Table I. Also good are the aircraft forecasts broadcast from some airports: frequencies and locations of these are listed on the Marine Weather Services Charts, which list storm warning display locations.

Tools for the weather-oriented navigator are simple and relatively inexpensive. Besides a radio receiver, he needs a good barometer aboard his boat and another, corrected to sea level, at home; a reliable anemometer (the hand-held type is adequate); and possibly a psychrometer. Where the pilot's house has an open wind flow on all sides, a combination wind vane-anemometer on the roof will help in establishing weather patterns before departure.

Afloat, barometer readings should be noted and logged every hour; significant wind shifts should also be logged. Complete forecasts should be made or obtained twice a day.

The following books should prove helpful: **Instant Weather Forecasting,** by Alan Watts (Dodd, Mead, & Company, 1968, out of print); **Weather for the Mariner** (second edition), by W.J. Kotsch (U.S. Naval Institute, 1977); **The Sager Weathercaster,** by R.M. Sager (Weather Publications, Pleasantville, N.Y., 1969. This book is part of a package that also contains a device for making one's own forecasts.); **Weather and Weather Forecasting,** by A.G. Forsdyke (Grosset and Dunlap, 1970, out of print); and **Mariner's Weather,** by W.P. Crawford (W.W. Norton & Company, Inc., 1978).

NOAA WEATHER ON VHF/FM RADIO

The nationwide network of National Weather Service VHF/FM stations transmitting continuous weather forecasts on three frequencies has grown tremendously in the past decade. Virtually every boatman is now within range of one such station, and many have access to two at once, especially if their VHF/FM antenna is a tall one. An additional function of National Oceanic and Atmospheric Administration (NOAA) weather radio stations is to provide direct warnings to citizens in case of nuclear attack or natural disaster. Broadcasts can normally be received up to about 40 miles from the transmitter site.

In most areas, taped messages are cycled every four to six minutes and are routinely revised every one to three hours throughout the 24-hour day. In case of a weather emergency, forecasters can and do interrupt the taped service to substitute special warning messages. Along with these warnings, forecasters can also transmit a special signal that will activate receivers designed to provide a weather alarm function.

Typically, a mariner can receive NOAA VHF/FM weather on one of two crystal-controlled, receive-only channels in his boat's VHF/FM transceiver, or by employing a specially designed weather radio, crystal-controlled or tunable. As a general rule, NOAA's three frequencies are slightly above the highest frequency found on commercial FM radio receivers.

Most NOAA weather transmitters operate on either 162.55 MHz or 162.4 MHz, and most VHF/FM transceivers contain crystals for both these frequencies. In areas where channel interference is a problem — for example, where three stations can be heard — one of the transmitters will operate on 162.475 MHz. Anyone buying a VHF transceiver or weather radio should check the accompanying list of stations to see which frequencies he will require. As far as I can tell, stations vary little in the quality of their information. Coastal stations are best, however, because they emphasize marine rather than terrestrial weather.

TABLE I. NOAA WEATHER RADIO NETWORK

SUMMER 1980

Legend — frequencies are
identified as follows:
(1) — 162.550 MHz;
(2) — 162.400 MHz;
(3) — 162.475 MHz.

Location	Frequency
Alabama	
Anniston	3
Birmingham	1
Demopolis	3
Dozier	1
Florence	3
Huntsville	2
Louisville	3
Mobile	1
Montgomery	2
Tuscaloosa	2
Alaska	
Anchorage	1
Cordova	1
Fairbanks	1
Homer	2
Juneau	1
Ketchikan	1
Kodiak	1
Nome	1
Petersburg	1
Seward	1
Sitka	2
Valdez	1
Wrangell	2
Yakutat	1
Arizona	
Flagstaff	2
Phoenix	1
Tucson	2
Yuma (P)	1
Arkansas	
Ash Flat	2
Fayetteville	3
Fort Smith	2
Gurdon	3
Jonesboro	1
Little Rock	1
Star City	2
Texarkana	1
California	
Bakersfield (P)	1
Barstow**	2
Coachella (P)	2
Crescent City/ Brookings, OR	1

Location	Frequency
Eureka	2
Fresno	2
Los Angeles	1
Merced	1
Monterey	2
Point Arena	2
Redding (P)	1
Sacramento	2
San Diego	2
San Francisco	1
San Luis Obispo (P)	1
Santa Barbara	2
Colorado	
Alamosa (P)*	3
Colorado Springs*	2
Denver	1
Grand Junction*	3
Greeley	1
Longmont	2
Pueblo	2
Sterling*	2
Connecticut	
Hartford	3
Meriden	2
New London	1
Delaware	
Lewes	1
District of Columbia	
Washington, D.C.	1
Florida	
Daytona Beach	2
Fort Myers	3
Gainesville	3
Jacksonville	1
Key West	2
Melbourne	1
Miami	1
Orlando	3
Panama City	1
Pensacola	2
Tallahassee	2
Tampa	1
West Palm Beach	2

Location	Frequency
Georgia	
Athens	2
Atlanta	1
Augusta	1
Chatsworth	2
Columbus	2
Macon	3
Pelham	1
Savannah	2
Waycross	3
Hawaii	
Hilo	1
Honolulu	1
Kokee	2
Mt. Haleakala	2
Waimanalo (R)	2
Idaho	
Boise	1
Lewiston (P)	1
Pocatello	1
Twin Falls	2
Illinois	
Champaign	1
Chicago	1
Marion*	3
Moline	1
Peoria	3
Rockford	3
Springfield	2
Indiana	
Evansville	1
Fort Wayne	1
Indianapolis	1
Lafayette	3
South Bend	2
Terre Haute	2
Iowa	
Cedar Rapids	3
Des Moines	1
Dubuque (P)	2
Fort Dodge**	2
Sioux City*	3
Waterloo*	1

Location	Frequency
Kansas	
Chanute	2
Colby	3
Concordia	1
Dodge City	3
Ellsworth	2
Topeka	3
Wichita	1
Kentucky	
Ashland	1
Bowling Green	2
Covington	1
Elizabethtown (R)	2
Hazard	3
Lexington	2
Louisville	3
Mayfield	3
Pikeville (R)	2
Somerset	1
Louisiana	
Alexandria	3
Baton Rouge	2
Buras	3
Lafayette	1
Lake Charles	2
Monroe	1
Morgan City	3
New Orleans	1
Shreveport	2
Maine	
Ellsworth	2
Portland	1
Maryland	
Baltimore	2
Hagerstown	3
Salisbury	2
Massachusetts	
Boston	3
Hyannis	1
Worcester	1
Michigan	
Alpena	1
Detroit	1
Flint	2
Grand Rapids	1
Houghton	2
Marquette	1
Onondaga	2
Sault Sainte Marie	1
Traverse City	2
Minnesota	
Duluth	1

Location	Frequency
International Falls	1
Mankato	2
Minneapolis	1
Rochester	3
Saint Cloud (P)	3
Thief River Falls	1
Willmar (P)	2
Mississippi	
Ackerman	3
Booneville	1
Bude	1
Columbia (R)	2
Gulfport	2
Hattiesburg	3
Inverness	1
Jackson	2
Meridian	1
Oxford	2
Missouri	
Camdenton	1
Columbia	2
Hannibal	3
Joplin/Carthage	1
Kansas City	1
St. Joseph	2
St. Louis	1
Sikeston	2
Springfield	2
Montana	
Billings	1
Butte	1
Glasgow	1
Great Falls	1
Havre (P)	2
Helena	2
Kalispell*	1
Miles City	2
Missoula	2
Nebraska	
Bassett	3
Grand Island	2
Holdrege	3
Lincoln	3
Merriman	2
Norfolk	1
North Platte	1
Omaha	2
Scottsbluff	1
Nevada	
Elko	1
Ely	2
Las Vegas	1
Reno	1
Winnemucca	2

Location	Frequency
New Hampshire	
Concord	2
New Jersey	
Atlantic City	2
New Mexico	
Albuquerque	2
Clovis	3
Des Moines	1
Farmington	3
Hobbs	2
Las Cruces	2
Ruidoso	1
Santa Fe	1
New York	
Albany	1
Binghamton	3
Buffalo	1
Elmira	1
Kingston	3
New York City	1
Rochester	2
Syracuse	1
North Carolina	
Asheville	2
Cape Hatteras	1
Charlotte	3
Fayetteville	3
New Bern	2
Raleigh/Durham	1
Rocky Mount	3
Wilmington	1
Winston-Salem	2
North Dakota	
Bismarck	2
Dickinson*	2
Fargo	2
Jamestown*	2
Minot	2
Petersburg	2
Williston*	2
Ohio	
Akron	2
Caldwell	3
Cleveland	1
Columbus	1
Dayton	3
Lima	2
Sandusky	2
Toledo	1
Oklahoma	
Clinton	3
Enid	3

4

Location	Frequency	Location	Frequency	Location	Frequency
Lawton	1	**South Dakota**		**Utah**	
McAlester	3	Aberdeen*	3	Logan	2
Oklahoma City	2	Huron	1	Milford	2
Tulsa	1	Pierre	2	Roosevelt	2
		Rapid City*	1	Salt Lake City	1
Oregon		Sioux Falls	2		
Astoria	2			**Vermont**	
Coos Bay	2	**Tennessee**		Burlington	2
Eugene	2	Bristol	1	Windsor	3
Klamath Falls	1	Chattanooga	1		
Medford	2	Cookville	2	**Virginia**	
Newport	1	Jackson	1	Heathsville	2
Pendleton	1	Knoxville	3	Lynchburg	2
Portland	1	Memphis	3	Norfolk	1
Redmond	3	Nashville	1	Richmond	3
Roseburg	3	Shelbyville	3	Roanoke	3
Salem	3	Waverly	2		
				Washington	
Pennsylvania		**Texas**		Neah Bay	1
Allentown	2	Abilene	2	Seattle	1
Clearfield	1	Amarillo	1	Spokane	1
Erie	2	Austin	2	Wenatchee	3
Harrisburg	1	Beaumont(P)	3	Yakima	1
Johnstown	2	Big Spring	3		
Philadelphia	3	Brownsville	1	**West Virginia**	
Pittsburgh	1	Bryan	1	Charleston	2
Wilkes-Barre	1	Corpus Christi	1	Clarksburg	1
Williamsport (P)	2	Dallas	2		
		Del Rio	2	**Wisconsin**	
Puerto Rico		El Paso	1	Green Bay	1
San Juan	2	Fort Worth	1	LaCrosse (P)	1
Maricao*	1	Galveston	1	Madison	1
		Houston	2	Menominee	2
Rhode Island		Laredo	3	Milwaukee	2
Providence	2	Lubbock	2	Wausau	3
		Lufkin	1		
South Carolina		Midland	2	**Wyoming**	
Beaufort	3	Paris	1	Casper*	1
Charleston	1	Pharr	2	Cheyenne	3
Columbia	2	San Angelo	1	Lander*	3
Florence	1	San Antonio	1	Rawlins**	2
Greenville	1	Sherman	3	Rock Springs**	1
Myrtle Beach	2	Tyler	3	Sheridan (P)*	3
Sumter (R)	3	Victoria	2		
		Waco	3		
		Wichita Falls	3		

NOTES:

1. Stations marked with an asterisk (*) should be in operation prior to or during Spring 1980. Stations marked with double asterisk (**), indefinite delays.

2. Stations marked (R) are low powered experimental repeater stations serving a very limited local area.

3. Stations marked (P) operate less than 24 hours/day; however, hours are extended when possible during severe weather.

4. Occasionally the frequency of an existing or planned station must be changed because of unexpected radio frequency interference with adjacent NOAA Weather Radio stations and/or with other government or commercial operators within the area.

5. The list of operating stations is updated periodically. For a current list please write: NOAA, National Weather Service, 8060 13th Street, Silver Spring, MD 20910, Attn: W112.

BAROMETRIC VARIATION

"Normal" barometric pressure is generally accepted to be:

29.92 inches of mercury, or
1013.25 millibars.

The two types of barometers, mercurial and aneroid, are subject to variations deriving from their construction. Virtually all pleasure craft use aneroid barometers, which require correction only for index error and altitude. The latter is usually not a factor on pleasure boats; the former is peculiar to the individual instrument and changes with age. To keep track of the index error, compare the aneroid barometer at regular intervals to a corrected mercurial barometer. Aneroid barometers also require temperature correction, but this is normally built into the instrument.

Barometric Altitude Correction		
Ht. above sea level (ft.)	Factor added to reading to obtain sea level equivalence	
	Inches	Millibars
5	0.01	0.3
10	0.01	0.3
15	0.02	0.7
20	0.02	0.7
25	0.03	1.0

Diurnal variation (Figure 1) is the regular pattern of daily pressure changes resulting from the effects of atmospheric tides. In middle latitudes in winter, there is no observable pattern, but in summer (and in lower latitudes throughout the year) there is a regular diurnal variation, normally ranging from about one millibar (.03 inch) in middle and higher latitudes to two or three millibars in the tropics.

Maximum barometric pressures from diurnal variation are usually recorded at 1000 and 2200, local time; minimum readings (all other things being equal) are at 0400 and 1600.

The distance of a storm center from your position may be roughly determined by noting the rate at which the barometer is falling.

Rate of fall (Inches per hour)	Distance of storm center (Miles)
.04	250
.06	200
.08	125
.09	100
.10	90
.11	80
.12	70
Over .12	60 or less

TABLE II. BAROMETRIC CONVERSION: INCHES TO MILLIBARS

Inches	+.00	+.02	+.04	+.06	+.08
	Millibars	*Millibars*	*Millibars*	*Millibars*	*Millibars*
27.5	931.3	931.9	932.6	933.3	934.0
27.6	934.6	935.3	936.0	936.7	937.4
27.7	938.0	938.7	939.4	940.1	940.7
27.8	941.4	942.1	942.8	943.4	944.1
27.9	944.8	945.5	946.2	946.8	947.2
28.0	948.2	948.9	949.5	950.2	950.9
28.1	951.6	952.3	952.9	953.6	954.3
28.2	955.0	955.6	956.3	957.0	957.7
28.3	958.3	959.0	959.7	960.4	961.1
28.4	961.7	962.4	963.1	963.8	964.4
28.5	965.1	965.8	966.5	967.2	967.8
28.6	968.5	969.2	969.9	970.5	971.2
28.7	971.9	972.6	973.2	973.9	974.6
28.8	975.3	976.0	976.6	977.3	978.0
28.9	978.7	979.3	980.0	980.7	981.4
29.0	982.1	982.7	983.4	984.1	984.8
29.1	985.4	986.1	986.8	987.5	988.1
29.2	988.8	989.5	990.2	990.9	991.5
29.3	992.2	992.9	993.6	994.2	994.9
29.4	995.6	996.3	997.0	997.6	998.3
29.5	999.0	999.7	1000.3	1001.0	1001.7
29.6	1002.4	1003.0	1003.7	1004.4	1005.1
29.7	1005.8	1006.4	1007.1	1007.8	1008.5
29.8	1009.1	1009.8	1010.5	1011.2	1011.9
29.9	1012.5	1013.2	1013.9	1014.6	1015.2
30.0	1015.9	1016.6	1017.3	1017.9	1018.6
30.1	1019.3	1020.0	1020.7	1021.3	1022.0
30.2	1022.7	1023.4	1024.0	1024.7	1025.4
30.3	1026.1	1026.8	1027.4	1028.1	1028.8
30.4	1029.5	1030.1	1030.8	1031.5	1032.2
30.5	1032.8	1033.5	1034.2	1034.9	1035.6
30.6	1036.2	1036.9	1037.6	1038.3	1038.9
30.7	1039.6	1040.3	1041.0	1041.7	1042.3
30.8	1043.0	1043.7	1044.4	1045.0	1045.7
30.9	1046.4	1047.1	1047.7	1048.4	1049.1

Figure 1. Example of a local diurnal barometric variation

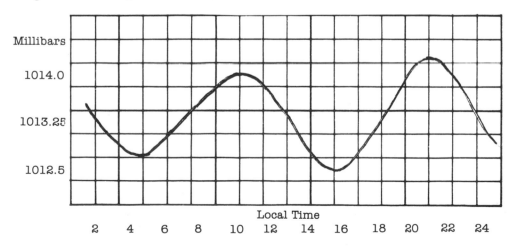

AIR MASSES

The earth's rotation — coupled with the heating, rising, and diffusion of air — is a major factor in the creation of prevailing winds, which are mostly from the west in the United States. There are, of course, variables to complicate the picture and cause the creation of air masses, which in turn condition our weather. There are two kinds of air mass:

- High-pressure areas, or **highs,** are formed when a mass of air cools (for any of a number of reasons), compresses, and sinks. Although an occasional very large high may cover most of the U.S., 200 to 2,000 miles is the usual size range. In the northern hemisphere, the relatively compressed air in a high circulates clockwise and outward, in a spiral. Most highs are inclined to move southeastward with the general progress of weather, but there are several semipermanent highs — the Pacific High, off the West Coast of the United States, and the Bermuda High, off the East Coast, for instance — usually formed over water. Fair weather, light winds, and stable temperatures are characteristic of high-pressure areas.

- Low-pressure masses, or **lows,** are in most respects the opposite of highs: they are formed as air heats and rises, lowering the barometric pressure. Surrounding air moves into a low, spiraling inward in a counterclockwise direction in the northern hemisphere. Lows are generally the source of bad weather, with strong winds and precipitation; the typical localized low is a thunderstorm, in which air rises at tremendous speed, creating violent weather in its wake.

Since lows move from west to east, and since they are associated with bad weather, your forecasting can be helped by knowing where a low is in relation to you. A principle called Buys-Ballot's Law can be applied here: stand with your back to the wind at ground level and turn about 45° to the right. This will normally align you with the wind aloft. As a rule, the nearest high-pressure mass is to your right, and the center of the low is to your left. Whichever air mass is to the west of you is on the way, while the one to the east has already passed.

Warm Front Weather Sequence

Warm fronts are usually located on the east side of a low-pressure system, often followed by pursuing cold fronts. Advance notice of the arrival of a warm front is even more long-term than suggested in the vertical cross section in Figure 2: the first banners of cloud may be as much as 1,000 miles — two days — ahead of the frontal surface.

High cirrus clouds are the first to appear. They represent that part of the warm air mass that has been pushed highest and farthest up the retreating slope of cool air.

The cirrus clouds begin to thicken and lower, becoming cirrostratus. Cirrocumulus clouds, or mackerel sky, may appear, warning of unstable

8

Figure 2. Arrival of a warm front.

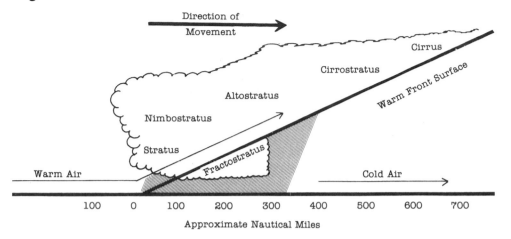

air aloft and possible thunderstorms. The barometer begins a steady fall and the winds begin to increase. Cirrostratus clouds now change to altostratus, and precipitation begins, continuing up to or beyond the time of frontal passage. The barometer continues to fall.

As the front nears, precipitation may stop; the clouds overhead are scud (fractostratus) and nimbostratus. As the front passes there is a clockwise shift of the wind, which may also decrease in strength. Visibility is poor, often in fog, and there is a continuing, steady temperature rise.

Behind the front are stratus or stratocumulus clouds and perhaps a light rain. Barometric pressure, which leveled as the front passed, may rise and then fall slightly. Fog or mist may remain, and the wind continues steady.

After the front has completely passed, the skies should clear and the wind will often be in the southwest. The ending of a warm front is considerably more abrupt than its arrival, but there may be a cold front approaching fairly quickly.

Cold Front Weather Sequence

Cold fronts are the easterly and southerly edges of cold air masses, moving at speeds of 10 to 50 knots (two or three times faster in winter than in summer). Since cold air is heavier than warm air, cold fronts tend to thrust themselves under the warm air ahead. Ground friction slows the advance of the cold air near the earth's surface, so the frontal surface has a reverse curve at the bottom, as shown in Figure 3, which is of course distorted vertically.

As the cold front moves (east or southeast), it lifts the air before it quite rapidly, so that the storms associated with cold front passage tend to be more violent than those attending a warm front. If a cold front is moving fast, it may be preceded by a squall line, a rolling boil of black, threatening clouds that may tower to 40,000 feet, containing violent thunderstorms and even tornadoes. The wind will shift suddenly and increase very quickly, and there will be torrential rain just behind the edge of the squall.

9

Figure 3. Arrival of a cold front

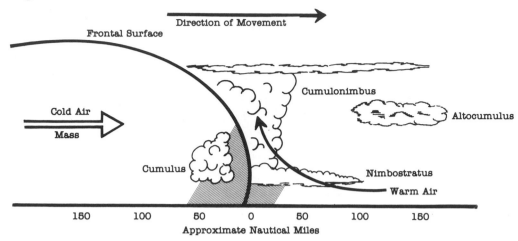

Ahead of a normal cold front, there will usually be rain, perhaps thunderstorms. Altocumulus and/or altostratus clouds are followed fairly quickly by nimbostratus, then heavy cumulonimbus. The barometer begins to fall, perhaps rapidly. The wind increases and becomes gusty.

The rain continues to fall, the wind increases, and the barometer drops still more. As the front passes, the winds shift clockwise very rapidly, continuing gusty; the barometer hits bottom, then begins a rapid rise as the temperature takes an equally sudden drop.

There will probably be heavy rain for a short period after the passage of the front, followed by rapid lifting of the clouds and gusty west or northwest winds. Pressure continues to rise and temperature to fall, but slowly. At least a couple of days of good weather should now ensue.

TABLE III. BAROMETRIC PRESSURE, WIND DIRECTION, AND FORECASTING

This table relates wind direction to barometric pressure and tendency, to produce a rough forecast. Generally speaking, three successive, hourly observations of a barometer will serve to establish its tendency.

Wind Direction	Pressure at Sea Level	Weather trend
SW to NW	30.10-30.20 Steady	Fair, little temperature change for one or two days.
SW to NW	30.10-30.20 Rising fast	Fair, followed by rain within two days.
SW to NW	30.20 or higher Steady	Continued fair; no marked temperature change.
SW to NW	30.20 or higher Falling slowly	Fair for two days; slowly rising temperature.

10

Continued

Wind Direction	Pressure at Sea Level	Weather trend
S to SE	30.10-30.20 Falling slowly	Rain within 24 hours.
S to SE	30.10-30.20 Falling fast	Increasing winds; rain in 12 to 24 hours.
SE to NE	30.10-30.20 Falling slowly	Increasing winds; rain within 12 to 18 hours.
SE to NE	30.10-30.20 Falling fast	Increasing winds; rain within 12 hours.
SE to NE	30.00 or below Falling slowly	Rain continuing one to three days or longer.
SE to NE	30.00 or below Falling fast	Rain, high winds within a few hours; clearing and cooler within 36 hours.
E to NE	30.10 or higher Falling slowly	In summer, with light winds, rain may not fall for two or three days; in winter, rain within 24 hours.
E to NE	30.10 or higher Falling fast	In summer, rain probably within 12 to 24 hours; in winter, rain or snow, increasing winds, within 12 hours.
E to N	29.80 or below Falling fast	Severe storm within a few hours; heavy rain or snow.
S to E	29.80 or below Falling fast	Severe storm within a few hours, then clearing within 24 hours.
S to SW	30.00 or below Rising slowly	Clearing within a few hours; fair for several days.

Falling fast or Rising fast means a pressure change of .24 inch or more within three hours. Falling slowly or Rising slowly means a change of approximately .09 inch or less in a three-hour period.

TABLE IV. CLOUD FORMATIONS

DESCRIPTION	PORTENT

High Clouds — 18,000 to 45,000 feet

Cirrus (ci): strands or fibers of high, white cloud, formed of ice crystals. Often arranged in bands called "mares' tails."	If scattered and not increasing, little immediate weather meaning. Ci in thick patches indicates showers nearby, often associated with thunderstorms. Ci shaped like hooks or commas suggest an approaching warm front with associated continuous rain.

Continued

DESCRIPTION	PORTENT
Cirrostratus (cs): transparent whitish clouds in a veil or film-like formation. Do not obscure the sun.	Cs in a continuous sheet, especially following ci, indicates approaching warm front or occluded front, with consequent rain. Possible halo effect around sun.
Cirrocumulus (cc): grainy, rippled sheets, patches, or layers of cloud with slight vertical development. When uniformly arranged in ripple shapes, they are called "mackerel sky."	Quite rare, with mixed meanings. Often indicate good weather in New England and the West Coast of the U.S. When seen as part of an approaching cold front pattern, however, cc may indicate thunderstorms.

Middle Clouds — 6,500 to 18,000 feet

DESCRIPTION	PORTENT
Altostratus (as): thick veil or layer of gray cloud covering all or part of the sky. Sun or moon just visible through as.	Almost always indicates coming, long-term rain or snow. Frequently means a stormy low-pressure system is developing at some distance.
Altocumulus (ac): even layers or sheets of fairly dense cloud. Resembles ripply pattern of cc above.	Have most meaning as transitional phase followed by thicker low clouds, or developing vertically, indicating possible thunderstorm.

Low Clouds — near ground to 6,500 feet

DESCRIPTION	PORTENT
Nimbostratus (ns): low, dark rain-bearing clouds, often accompanied by wind-driven scud.	Prolonged rain or snow; fresh to strong winds.
Stratus (st): low, gray layers or sheets of cloud; sky has a leaden appearance.	Damp, possible drizzle. If wind decreases sharply, fog may develop.
Stratocumulus (sc): irregular patchy layers of cloud; looks like ac, but lower, more distinct.	Usually followed by clearing at night and subsequent fair weather.

12

Vertical Clouds — near ground to 45,000 feet

Cumulus **(cu)**: well-defined, fleecy puffs, changing shape. White at top, dark at base.	When detached and puffy, indicate fair weather. With substantial vertical development, showers and gusty winds.
Cumulonimbus **(cb)**: heavy, dark towers; anvil top or plume.	Thunderheads: gusty winds, rain, hail, lightning.

FREEHAND WEATHER FORECASTING

Different people have different approaches to predicting the local weather, but whatever the method (short of consulting the entrails of a sheep), it all amounts to the same thing: accumulating enough indicators to shape a trend. The categories that follow are composed of easily observable phenomena. Two or (better) three mutually agreeing clues will usually be a reliable signpost to the coming weather in your immediate area. Bear in mind, however, that weather observation is not a momentary occupation: your readings — even these freehand ones — should be continuous throughout the day.

Deteriorating weather indicated by:

   Clouds lowering and thickening.
   Clouds increasing in number, moving rapidly across the sky.
   Ac or **as** clouds on the western horizon.
   Clouds moving in different directions at different heights.
   Clouds moving from NE or E to S.
   Scud clouds under heavy cloud masses.
   Distant clouds breaking into streaks, then forming murk.
   Barometer falling steadily.
   Barometer falling rapidly, with **as** or **ac** clouds in W.
   Static on AM radio.
   Wind shifts from N to E and/or through E to S.
   Strong wind in the morning.
   Temperatures far above or below normal for time of year.

Wind indicators:

   Light scud clouds alone in clear sky.
   The sharper and better defined the cloud, the more wind.
   Yellow sunset means increasing wind.
   Unusually bright stars mean increased wind.
   High clouds' movement suggests future wind direction.

Precipitation indicated by:

Distant objects seeming to stand above horizon.
Sounds are extra clear, heard for long distances.
When **cs** clouds begin to thicken and lower, rain within 20-40 hours.
Cs clouds seen with sun or moon halo, rain in 12-24 hours.
Increasing southerly wind with clouds moving from W.
Wind (especially northerly) shifts to W, then to S.
Steadily falling barometer.
Pale sunset.
Hot morning sun breaking through clouds.
Red sky at dawn.
No dew after hot day.

Fog-producing conditions (see also Table V):

Clear at sunset, light wind, high humidity.
Warm rain falling through colder air.
Warm water with cold air blowing above.
Warm southerly wind over cold land or water.

Clearing weather indicators:

Cloud bases rise.
Clearing sky. Clouds dissipate.
Wind shifts to W, especially from E, through S.
Barometer rises rapidly.
Gray early morning.
Morning fog or dew.

Continuing fair weather:

Early morning summer fog clears.
Decreasing number of clouds.
Gentle wind from W or NW.
Normal temperatures for time of year.
Barometer steady or rising slowly.
Red sunset.
Bright moon, light wind.
Heavy dew or frost.
Clear, bright blues in morning sky.
Dull hearing, short range of sound.

Weather Jingles

Among the oldest and most familiar rhymes are the traditional ones having to do with coming weather — in part their survival is due to their practicality, as an easy way to memorize key indicators. Here are some of the more reliable and less obscure rhymes:

Red sky at night, sailor's delight;
Red in the morning, sailors take warning.

If the wind's before the rain, soon you may make sail again.
If the rain's before the wind, topsails lower, halyards mind.

Long foretold, long last.
Short notice, soon past.

When mist takes to the open sea,
Fair-weather shipmate it will be.

At sea, with low and falling glass,
Soundly sleeps the careless ass.
Only when it's high and risin'
Soundly sleeps the careful wise 'un.

The farther the sight, the nearer the rain.

When sound travels far and wide,
A stormy day will like betide.

First rise* after low
Indicates a stronger blow.

*of the barometer.

FOG FORECASTING

By the use of a sling psychrometer (containing dry- and wet-bulb ther-
mometers) and Table V, the likelihood of fog may be predicted with
reasonable accuracy.
   Subtract the reading of the wet-bulb thermometer in degrees Fahrenheit
from that of the dry-bulb. Enter the left-hand column of the table with the
difference between the two readings. Now enter the top of the table in the
column most closely corresponding to the air temperature (shown on the
dry-bulb thermometer). The intersection of the horizontal line (dry-bulb
minus wet-bulb) and the vertical column (dry-bulb temperature) will give
an estimate of the air temperature–dew point spread in degrees
Fahrenheit.
   If it is early evening or late afternoon; and if the air temperature is falling; and if the air temperature–dew point spread is less than approximately 6°, then fog or restricted visibility is likely within the next few hours.

TABLE V. DEW POINT

Dry-Bulb minus Wet-bulb	Air Temperature (Dry-Bulb Thermometer)												
	35	40	45	50	55	60	65	70	75	80	85	90	95
1	2	2	2	2	2	2	2	1	1	1	1	1	1
2	5	5	4	4	4	3	3	3	3	3	3	3	2
3	7	7	7	6	5	5	5	4	4	4	4	4	4
4	10	10	9	8	7	7	6	6	6	6	5	5	5
5	14	12	11	10	10	9	8	8	7	7	7	7	6
6	18	15	14	13	12	11	10	9	9	8	8	8	8
7	22	19	17	16	14	13	12	11	11	10	10	9	9
8	28	22	20	18	17	15	14	13	12	12	11	11	10
9	35	27	23	21	19	17	16	15	14	13	13	12	12
10	--	33	27	24	22	20	18	17	16	15	14	14	13
11	--	40	32	28	25	22	20	19	18	17	16	15	15
12	--	--	38	32	28	25	23	21	20	18	17	17	16
13	--	--	45	37	31	28	25	23	21	20	19	18	17
14	--	--	--	42	35	31	28	26	24	22	21	20	19
15	--	--	--	50	40	35	31	28	26	24	23	21	21

To find the dew point, subtract the spread figure in the table from the air temperature (dry-bulb thermometer). **Example:** If the temperature registers 70° on the dry-bulb thermometer and 59° on the wet-bulb, the difference between the two readings is 11°. This gives a tabular spread of 19°, which, subtracted from 70°, yields a dew point of 51°.

If the air temperature is 76° and the wet-bulb reading is 73°, the difference is 3°. Using the table, this figure produces an air temperature-dew point spread of 4°, suggesting that fog or diminished visibility is imminent.

WINDCHILL FACTOR

Table VI combines true air temperature, in degrees Fahrenheit, with wind velocity, in miles per hour, to give the effective temperature. The graph is based on the fact that two of the three primary forms of heat loss, radiation and conduction, are relatively constant for a given combination of wind velocity and air temperature.

For example, in a 25 m.p.h. wind, a temperature of 20 degrees Fahrenheit has the same cooling effect as would one of − 15° Fahrenheit with no wind present.

The effects on a given individual will, of course, vary with his personal health, the amount of recent physical exertion, and the presence or absence of sunshine.

TABLE VI. WINDCHILL FACTORS

Dry-Bulb Temperature (°F)

	45	40	35	30	25	20	15	10	5	0	−5	−10	−15	−20	−25	−30	−35	−40	−45	
4	45	40	35	30	25	20	15	10	5	0	−5	−10	−15	−20	−25	−30	−35	−40	−45	4
5	43	37	32	27	22	16	11	6	0	−5	−10	−15	−21	−26	−31	−36	−42	−47	−52	5
10	34	28	22	16	10	3	−3	−9	−15	−22	−27	−34	−40	−46	−52	−58	−64	−71	−77	10
15	29	23	16	9	2	−5	−11	−18	−25	−31	−38	−45	−51	−58	−65	−72	−78	−85	−92	15
20	26	19	12	4	−3	−10	−17	−24	−31	−39	−46	−53	−60	−67	−74	−81	−88	−95	−103	20
25	23	16	8	1	−7	−15	−22	−29	−36	−44	−51	−59	−66	−74	−81	−88	−96	−103	−110	25
30	21	13	6	−2	−10	−18	−25	−33	−41	−49	−56	−64	−71	−79	−86	−93	−101	−109	−116	30
35	20	12	4	−4	−12	−20	−27	−35	−43	−52	−58	−67	−74	−82	−89	−97	−105	−113	−120	35
40	19	11	3	−5	−13	−21	−29	−37	−45	−53	−60	−69	−76	−84	−92	−100	−107	−115	−123	40
45	18	10	2	−6	−14	−22	−30	−38	−46	−54	−62	−70	−78	−85	−93	−102	−109	−117	−125	45

Wind Velocity (MPH)

TABLE VII. TEMPERATURE CONVERSION: Degrees Fahrenheit to Degrees Celsius (Centigrade)

F	C	F	C	F	C	F	C
00	−17.7	10	−12.2	20	− 6.7	30	− 1.1
00.5	−17.5	10.5	−11.9	20.5	− 6.4	30.5	− 0.8
01	−17.2	11	−11.7	21	− 6.1	31	− 0.6
01.5	−16.9	11.5	−11.4	21.5	− 5.8	31.5	− 0.3
02	−16.7	12	−11.1	22	− 5.6	32	0.0
02.5	−16.4	12.5	−10.8	22.5	− 5.3	32.5	0.3
03	−16.1	13	−10.6	23	− 5.0	33	0.6
03.5	−15.8	13.5	−10.3	23.5	− 4.7	33.5	0.8
04	−15.6	14	−10.0	24	− 4.4	34	1.1
04.5	−15.3	14.5	− 9.7	24.5	− 4.2	34.5	1.4
05	−15.0	15	− 9.4	25	− 3.9	35	1.7
05.5	−14.7	15.5	− 9.2	25.5	− 3.6	35.5	1.9
06	−14.4	16	− 8.9	26	− 3.3	36	2.2
06.5	−14.2	16.5	− 8.6	26.5	− 3.1	36.5	2.5
07	−13.9	17	− 8.3	27	− 2.8	37	2.8
07.5	−13.6	17.5	− 8.1	27.5	− 2.5	37.5	3.1
08	−13.3	18	− 7.8	28	− 2.2	38	3.3
08.5	−13.1	18.5	− 7.5	28.5	− 1.9	38.5	3.6
09	−12.8	19	− 7.2	29	− 1.7	39	3.9
09.5	−12.5	19.5	− 6.9	29.5	− 1.4	39.5	4.2

Continued

17

F	C	F	C	F	C	F	C
40	4.4	55	12.8	70	21.1	85	29.4
40.5	4.7	55.5	13.1	70.5	21.4	85.5	29.7
41	5.0	56	13.3	71	21.7	86	30.0
41.5	5.3	56.5	13.6	71.5	21.9	86.5	30.3
42	5.6	57	13.9	72	22.2	87	30.6
42.5	5.8	57.5	14.2	72.5	22.5	87.5	30.8
43	6.1	58	14.4	73	22.8	88	31.1
43.5	6.4	58.5	14.7	73.5	23.1	88.5	31.4
44	6.7	59	15.0	74	23.3	89	31.7
44.5	6.9	59.5	15.3	74.5	23.6	89.5	31.9
45	7.2	60	15.6	75	23.9	90	32.2
45.5	7.5	60.5	15.8	75.5	24.2	90.5	32.5
46	7.8	61	16.1	76	24.4	91	32.8
46.5	8.1	61.5	16.4	76.5	24.7	91.5	33.1
47	8.3	62	16.7	77	25.0	92	33.3
47.5	8.6	62.5	16.9	77.5	25.3	92.5	33.6
48	8.9	63	17.2	78	25.6	93	33.9
48.5	9.2	63.5	17.5	78.5	25.8	93.5	34.2
49	9.4	64	17.8	79	26.1	94	34.4
49.5	9.7	64.5	18.1	79.5	26.4	94.5	34.7
50	10.0	65	18.3	80	26.7	95	35.0
50.5	10.3	65.5	18.6	80.5	26.9	95.5	35.3
51	10.6	66	18.9	81	27.2	96	35.6
51.5	10.8	66.5	19.2	81.5	27.5	96.5	35.8
52	11.1	67	19.4	82	27.8	97	36.1
52.5	11.4	67.5	19.7	82.5	28.1	97.5	36.4
53	11.7	68	20.0	83	28.3	98	36.7
53.5	11.9	68.5	20.3	83.5	28.6	98.5	36.9
54	12.2	69	20.6	84	28.9	99	37.2
54.5	12.5	69.5	20.8	84.5	29.2	99.5	37.5

DIRECTION AND SPEED OF TRUE WIND

Table VIII provides a means of converting apparent wind, observed aboard a vessel underway, to true wind. To use the table, divide the apparent wind (in knots) by the vessel's speed, also in knots. This gives the apparent wind speed in units of ship's speed. Enter the table with this value and the difference between the ship's heading and the apparent wind direction. The values taken from the table are: (a) the difference between the heading and the true wind direction, and (b) the speed of the wind in units of ship's speed. The true wind is on the same side as the apparent wind, and from some point farther aft.

To convert the wind speed from units of ship's speed to speed in knots, multiply by the vessel's speed in knots. The steadiness of the wind and the accuracy of its measurement are seldom sufficient to warrant interpolation in this table. If the speed of the true wind and the relative direction of the apparent wind are known, enter the column for direction of the apparent wind, and find the speed of the true wind in units of ship's speed. The number to the left is the relative direction of the true wind. The number on the same line in the side column is the speed of the apparent wind in units of ship's speed. Two solutions are possible if speed of the true wind is less than the ship's speed.

18

Example: A vessel is heading 030 T at 8 knots. The apparent wind is 12 knots, from a direction 050 T. To convert the apparent wind speed to units of ship's speed, divide 12 knots by 8 knots; the result is 1.5. Now find the difference between the apparent wind direction (050) and the ship's heading (030); the result is 20°.

Enter the left side of the table at line 1.5 and the top of the table at 20°. The intersection yields two figures: 051 and 0.66. Add 051 to the ship's heading (030) to find the true wind direction, 081 T. Multiply the vessel speed (8 knots) by 0.66 to find the true wind speed, 5.3 knots.

TABLE VIII. DIRECTION AND SPEED OF TRUE WIND IN UNITS OF SHIP'S SPEED (from Bowditch)

Apparent wind speed	Difference between the heading and apparent wind direction									
	0°		10°		20°		30°		40°	
0.0	180	1.00	180	1.00	180	1.00	180	1.00	180	1.00
0.5	180	0.50	170	0.51	162	0.56	156	0.62	152	0.70
1.0	calm	0.00	095	0.17	100	0.35	105	0.52	110	0.68
1.5	000	0.50	029	0.54	051	0.66	068	0.81	081	0.98
2.0	000	1.00	020	1.03	038	1.11	054	1.24	068	1.39
2.5	000	1.50	017	1.52	032	1.60	047	1.71	060	1.85
3.0	000	2.00	015	2.02	029	2.09	043	2.19	056	2.32
3.5	000	2.50	014	2.52	028	2.58	041	2.68	053	2.81
4.0	000	3.00	013	3.02	026	3.08	039	3.17	051	3.30
4.5	000	3.50	013	3.52	025	3.58	038	3.67	050	3.79
5.0	000	4.00	012	4.02	025	4.08	037	4.16	049	4.28
6.0	000	5.00	012	5.02	024	5.07	036	5.16	047	5.27
7.0	000	6.00	012	6.02	023	6.07	035	6.15	046	6.27
8.0	000	7.00	011	7.02	023	7.07	034	7.15	045	7.26
9.0	000	8.00	011	8.02	022	8.07	034	8.15	044	8.26
10.0	000	9.00	011	9.02	022	9.06	033	9.15	044	9.26

	50°		60°		70°		80°		90°	
0.0	180	1.00	180	1.00	180	1.00	180	1.00	180	1.00
0.5	151	0.78	150	0.87	150	0.95	152	1.04	153	1.12
1.0	115	0.85	120	1.00	125	1.15	130	1.29	135	1.41
1.5	092	1.15	101	1.32	109	1.49	117	1.65	124	1.80
2.0	079	1.56	090	1.73	100	1.91	108	2.07	117	2.24
2.5	072	2.01	083	2.18	094	2.35	103	2.53	112	2.69
3.0	068	2.48	079	2.65	089	2.82	099	2.99	108	3.16
3.5	065	2.96	076	3.12	087	3.29	096	3.47	106	3.64
4.0	063	3.44	074	3.61	084	3.78	094	3.95	104	4.12
4.5	061	3.93	072	4.09	083	4.26	093	4.44	103	4.61
5.0	060	4.42	071	4.58	081	4.75	092	4.93	101	5.10
6.0	058	5.41	069	5.57	079	5.74	090	5.91	099	6.08
7.0	057	6.40	068	6.56	078	6.72	088	6.90	098	7.07
8.0	056	7.40	067	7.55	077	7.72	087	7.89	097	8.06
9.0	055	8.39	066	8.54	076	8.71	086	8.88	096	9.06
10.0	055	9.39	065	9.54	076	9.70	086	9.88	096	10.01

Continued

Apparent wind speed	Difference between the heading and apparent wind direction									
	100°		110°		120°		130°		140°	
0.0	180	1.00	180	1.00	180	1.00	180	1.00	180	1.00
0.5	156	1.19	158	1.26	161	1.32	164	1.38	167	1.42
1.0	140	1.53	145	1.64	150	1.73	155	1.81	160	1.88
1.5	130	1.94	137	2.07	143	2.18	150	2.28	156	2.36
2.0	124	2.39	132	2.52	139	2.65	146	2.75	153	2.84
2.5	120	2.85	128	2.99	136	3.12	144	3.23	151	3.33
3.0	117	3.32	126	3.47	134	3.61	142	3.72	150	3.82
3.5	115	3.80	124	3.96	132	4.09	140	4.21	149	4.31
4.0	113	4.29	122	4.44	131	4.58	139	4.71	148	4.81
4.5	112	4.78	121	4.93	130	5.07	138	5.20	147	5.31
5.0	111	5.27	120	5.42	129	5.57	138	5.69	146	5.80
6.0	109	6.25	118	6.41	128	6.56	137	6.69	145	6.80
7.0	108	7.24	117	7.40	127	7.55	136	7.68	145	7.79
8.0	107	8.23	116	8.39	126	8.54	135	8.68	144	8.79
9.0	106	9.23	116	9.39	125	9.54	135	9.67	144	9.79
10.0	106	10.22	115	10.39	125	10.54	134	10.67	143	10.78

	150°		160°		170°		180°	
0.0	180	1.00	180	1.00	180	1.00	180	1.00
0.5	170	1.45	173	1.48	177	1.50	180	1.50
1.0	165	1.93	170	1.97	175	1.99	180	2.00
1.5	162	2.42	168	2.46	174	2.49	180	2.50
2.0	160	2.91	167	2.96	173	2.99	180	3.00
2.5	158	3.40	166	3.46	173	3.49	180	3.50
3.0	157	3.90	165	3.95	172	3.99	180	4.00
3.5	157	4.39	164	4.45	172	4.49	180	4.50
4.0	156	4.89	164	4.95	172	4.99	180	5.00
4.5	155	5.39	164	5.45	172	5.49	180	5.50
5.0	155	5.89	163	5.95	172	5.99	180	6.00
6.0	154	6.88	163	6.95	171	6.99	180	7.00
7.0	154	7.88	162	7.95	171	7.99	180	8.00
8.0	153	8.88	162	8.95	171	8.99	180	9.00
9.0	153	9.88	162	9.95	171	9.99	180	10.00
10.0	153	10.88	162	10.95	171	10.98	180	11.00

TABLE IX. WIND SPEED SCALES AND EFFECTS AT SEA

Beaufort Number	Knots	Term	Effects Observed at Sea
0	- 1	Calm	Sea like a mirror
1	1-3	Light air	Ripples; no foam crests
2	4-6	Light breeze	Small wavelets; crests of glassy appearance, not breaking.
3	7-10	Gentle breeze	Large wavelets; crests begin to break; scattered whitecaps.
4	11-16	Moderate breeze	Small waves becoming larger; numerous whitecaps.
5	17-21	Fresh breeze	Moderate waves, taking longer form; many whitecaps, some spray; Small Craft Advisory may be hoisted.
6	22-27	Strong breeze	Larger waves forming; whitecaps everywhere; more spray.
7	28-33	Moderate gale	Sea heaps up; white foam from breaking waves begins to be blown in streaks.

Continued

Beaufort Number	Knots	Term	Effects Observed at Sea
8	34-40	Fresh gale	Moderately high waves of greater length; edges of crests begin to break into spindrift; foam blown in well-marked streaks; Gale or Tropical Storm Warnings hoisted.
9	41-47	Strong gale	High waves; seas begin to roll; dense streaks of foam; spray may reduce visibility.
10	48-55	Storm	Very high waves with overhanging crests; sea takes white appearance from foam blown in very dense streaks; rolling is heavy and visibility reduced. Storm Warnings hoisted.
11	56-63	Violent storm	Exceptionally high waves; sea covered with white foam patches; visibility still more reduced.
12	64-71	Hurricane	Air filled with foam; sea completely white with driving spray; visibility greatly reduced. Hurricane/Typhoon Warnings hoisted.
13-17	Although Beaufort Scale numbers exist for wind forces to 118 knots, they are of academic interest to the pleasure boatman.		

TABLE X. WIND SPEED SCALES AND EFFECTS ON LAND

Beaufort Number	MPH	Km/Hr	Effects Observed on Land	Approx. Weather Map Symbol
0	- 1	- 1	Smoke rises vertically.	◯
1	1-3	1-5	Smoke drifts; weathervanes still.	◯—
2	4-7	6-11	Wind felt on face; leaves rustle; weathervanes begin to move.	◯— (5 knots)
3	8-12	12-19	Leaves, small twigs in constant motion; light flags extended.	◯— (10 knots)
4	13-18	20-28	Dust, leaves and loose paper raised up; small branches move.	◯— (15 knots)
5	19-24	29-38	Small trees in leaf begin to sway.	◯— (20 knots)
6	25-31	39-49	Larger branches of trees in motion; whistling heard in wires.	◯— (25 knots)
7	32-38	50-61	Whole trees in motion; resistance felt walking against the wind.	◯— (30 knots)
8	39-46	62-74	Twigs and small branches blown off trees; progress generally impeded.	◯— (35 knots)
9	47-54	75-88	Slight structural damage occurs; slate or shingles blown off.	◯— (45 knots)
10	55-63	89-102	Seldom experienced on land; trees broken or uprooted; considerable structural damage occurs.	◯— (50 knots)
11	64-72	103-117	Very rarely experienced on land; usually accompanied by widespread damage.	◯— (60 knots)
12	73-82	118-133		◯— (65 knots)

WAVE HEIGHTS AND WIND FORCE

There are three factors in the description of a wave: its **height** from trough to crest; its **length** from one crest to the next; and its **period,** the time interval between the passage of one crest and the next at a fixed point. When the ratio of height to length (H/L) increases to 1/10 or 1/7 (authorities disagree), the wave becomes unstable.

For any given wind speed there is a maximum theoretical wave height, which in reality could only be attained if the fetch (the open-water distance over which the wind blows) were infinitely long. Some representative wind speeds and associated maximum wave heights are shown below. (Tables from W.J. Kotsch, **Weather for the Mariner,** U.S. Naval Institute, 1977.)

Wind Speed (Knots)	Wave Height (Feet)	Wind Speed (Knots)	Wave Height (Feet)
8	3	35	30
12	5	39	36
16	8	43	39
19	12	47	45
27	20	51	51
31	25		

With wind speed held constant, the relationship of wave height to actual fetch is described by the following table.

Wind Speed (Knots)	Fetch in Nautical Miles					
	10	50	100	300	500	1,000
10	2	2	2	2	2	2
15	3	4	5	5	5	5
20	4	7	8	9	9	9
30	6	13	16	18	19	20
40	8	18	23	30	33	34
50	10	22	30	44	47	51

Fetch aside, the heights of waves are also directly related to the length of time a wind of a given strength has been blowing, as the next table indicates.

Wind Speed (Knots)	Duration of Wind (Hours)						
	5	10	15	20	30	40	50
10	2	2	2	2	2	2	2
15	4	4	5	5	5	5	5
20	5	7	8	8	9	9	9
30	9	13	16	17	18	19	19
40	14	21	25	28	31	33	33
50	19	29	36	40	45	48	50
60	24	37	47	54	62	67	69

A wave's speed is normally related to the wind speed. When wind speeds are under 25 knots, wave speeds are usually slightly higher than wind speeds. When wind speeds are substantially over 25 knots, wave speeds are generally somewhat less than wind speeds. To find wave speed, the following formula is used:

$$\text{Wave speed (V)} = \frac{\text{Length (feet)}}{\text{Period (seconds)}} \times 0.6$$

VISUAL WEATHER WARNINGS AND WEATHER SERVICE CHARTS

Although there has been some controversy over their effectiveness in recent years, especially in view of the widespread use of NOAA continuous weather forecasts on VHF/FM radio (see opening section, Chapter One), the familiar warning flags and lights remain in use in many American harbors. They appear on structures whose proprietors — usually yacht clubs, marine police units, Coast Guard Auxiliary flotillas and marinas — have agreed to display the signals specified by the National Weather Service. In many areas, marine police patrol craft will also display the Small Craft Advisory pennant (see Figure 4) when winds of 18 knots or more are expected.

Locations of weather warning display stations in a given area are summarized on one of a series of charts issued by the National Weather Service and available from National Ocean Survey, Distribution Division (C44), Riverdale, MD 20840. Prices change from time to time, so call for information: (301) 344-2613. The current list of charts is as follows:

MSC - 1   Eastport, ME to Montauk Point, NY
MSC - 2   Montauk Point, NY to Manasquan, NJ
MSC - 3   Manasquan, NJ to Cape Hatteras, NC
MSC - 4   Cape Hatteras, NC to Savannah, GA
MSC - 5   Savannah, GA to Apalachicola, FL
MSC - 6   Apalachicola, FL to Morgan City, LA
MSC - 7   Morgan City, LA to Brownsville, TX
MSC - 8   Mexican Border to Pt. Conception, CA
MSC - 9   Pt. Conception, CA to Pt. St. George, CA
MSC - 10 Pt. St. George, CA to Canadian Border
MSC - 11 Lakes Michigan and Superior
MSC - 12 Lakes Huron, Erie, and Ontario
MSC - 13 Hawaiian waters
MSC - 14 Puerto Rico and Virgin Islands
MSC - 15 Alaskan waters

Besides listing marine weather displays, the weather charts give transmitter locations and approximate ranges for NOAA VHF/FM stations in the

23

area, and list some commercial stations that offer marine weather forecasts.

The following wind warning terms are used to describe closed cyclonic (rotary) circulation systems of tropical origin:

Tropical Depression =   Winds to 33 knots
Tropical Storm =   Winds 34-63 knots
Hurricane/Typhoon =   Winds 64 knots or more.

Winds of over 64 knots that are not associated with a closed, cyclonic system of tropical origin are covered by Storm Warnings. Marine Weather Warnings are as follows:

Small Craft Advisory = Winds to 33 knots/38 m.p.h.
Gale Warning =   Winds 34-47 knots/39-54 m.p.h.
Storm Warning =   Winds 48+ knots/55+ m.p.h.
Hurricane =   Winds 64+ knots/74+ m.p.h.

A small craft advisory, more specifically, indicates sustained (more than two hours) winds of 18 to 33 knots and/or seas hazardous to small craft.

Figure 4. Visual warnings

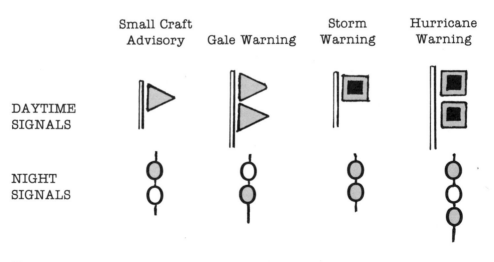

Note: black = black
      gray = red

2/ SPEED / TIME / DISTANCE

Of all the procedures involved in coastal navigation, figuring speed, time, and distance seems to involve the most personalized approaches. Some people with a knack for numbers prefer to work things out from scratch; others refer to tables, relying on the expertise of those who've gone before; still others employ dividers and a logarithmic scale; and many read an answer, hopefully correct, on a dial.

While it's impossible in a book this size to include every system, I have tried to present in some adequate form the most popular ones, especially those useful at low speeds where mechanical and electronic speedometers tend to err most. I trust your favorite system is in this section. If you haven't got a favorite — or even if you have — you may want to browse a bit or sample another method.

Tools required for calculating speed, time, and distance can be either simple and cheap or wildly complex and expensive. Personally, I haven't found any consistent correlation between cost and accuracy, except when cost has become stratospheric.

The average pilot will require (depending on his system) pencil, watch (with a sweep or stop second hand), dividers, a simple speed/time/distance calculator, and possibly a mechanical or electronic speedometer–log. He will find it most helpful to have a reliable record of his boat's speed through the water at different throttle settings, as provided for in this chapter. If he is a sailing skipper, he will accumulate a less easily recorded feel for her approximate speed through the water as revealed in hull noise and wave formation.

For those who use electronic speedometers, it's a good idea to post, alongside the instrument, a table of corrections for the main increments on the readout dial — or at least a simple notation that the machine always reads a knot too fast, or is useless at speeds below two knots, or exhibits any other idiosyncrasies.

Speed/time/distance calculations are basically pretty simple if you practice and don't get rattled. A book prepared for members of the U.S. Coast Guard Auxiliary entitled **Piloting and Dead Reckoning** can be recommended. It is written by H.H. Shufeldt and G.D. Dunlap (the authors of the 12th edition of **Dutton's Navigation and Piloting**) and is published by the U.S. Naval Institute.

SPEED/TIME/DISTANCE FORMULAS

As nearly everyone has learned at some time or other, the basic speed/time/distance formula is

$$D = \frac{S \times T}{60}$$

often transformed to 60D = ST, and remembered with the mnemonic "60 D Street." In the formula, D = distance in nautical or statute miles, S = speed over the ground in knots or land miles per hour, T = time in minutes. Variants of the first formula are:

$$T = \frac{60 D}{S} \text{, and} \quad S = \frac{60 D}{T}$$

USE OF THE LOGARITHMIC SCALE

Most charts have printed on them a logarithmic scale like the one reproduced above. Accompanying instructions tell how to find the ship's speed with the aid of dividers. The scale may also be used to compute either distance or time, when the other two are known.

To find **speed,** place one point of the dividers on miles run and the other on minutes run. Without changing the divider spread, place the right point on 60; the left point will then indicate speed. If the distance covered is in units of nautical miles, the speed will be in knots; if the miles run are statute, the speed will be in units of land miles per hour. For example, if 4.0 miles are run in 15 minutes, the speed is 16.0 m.p.h.

To find **time,** place the right leg of the dividers on 60 and the left leg on speed in nautical or statute miles per hour. Without changing the spread of the dividers, move them until the left leg indicates distance. The right leg position indicates time in minutes.

To find **distance,** place the right leg of the dividers on 60 and the left leg on speed in nautical or statute miles per hour. Maintaining the divider spread, move them until the right leg indicates time in minutes. The left leg now indicates distance in nautical or statute miles.

If the time is longer than one hour, solve the problem in hours and fractions thereof, rather than hours and minutes. For example, given a speed of 10 knots and a time of 2 hours 18 minutes, to find the distance run, place the left leg of the dividers on 1 and the right leg on 10. Maintaining the dividers' spread, place the left leg on 2.3; the right leg will indicate 23 (nautical miles).

THREE-MINUTE AND SIX-MINUTE RULES

In three minutes, a vessel underway moves a distance in hundreds of yards equal to her speed over the ground in knots. Or, put another way:

Speed x 100 = Yards traveled in 3 minutes

A boat's forward motion in a six-minute period equals her speed in knots divided by 10. Thus, a boat making four knots will travel 0.4 nautical mile in six minutes.

         3 knots – 100 yards a minute
         6 knots = 200 yards a minute
        15 knots = 500 yards a minute

SPEED / TIME / DISTANCE CONVERSION TABLES AND THEIR USE

Table XI will yield any single factor — speed over the ground, time, or distance — if you know the other two. It is scaled in half-knot increments, as this is a realistic interval for cruising boats. To find the speed in knots when you know the elapsed time and the distance run, enter the left- or right-hand vertical column with the time nearest to the elapsed time and move horizontally until you reach the distance run (in this case, units are nautical miles). The number at the top of the column is your boat's speed to the nearest half-knot.

TABLE XI. FINDING SPEED, TIME, OR DISTANCE

Min.	Speed in Knots/MPH															Min.
	0.5	1.0	1.5	2.0	2.5	3.0	3.5	4.0	4.5	5.0	5.5	6.0	6.5	7.0	7.5	
	Distance in Nautical/Statute Miles															
2	0.0	0.0	0.0	0.1	0.1	0.1	0.1	0.1	0.2	0.2	0.2	0.2	0.2	0.2	0.2	2
4	0.0	0.1	0.1	0.1	0.2	0.2	0.2	0.3	0.3	0.3	0.4	0.4	0.4	0.5	0.5	4
6	0.0	0.1	0.2	0.2	0.2	0.3	0.4	0.4	0.4	0.5	0.6	0.6	0.6	0.7	0.8	6
8	0.1	0.1	0.2	0.3	0.3	0.4	0.5	0.5	0.6	0.7	0.7	0.8	0.9	0.9	1.0	8
10	0.1	0.2	0.2	0.3	0.4	0.5	0.6	0.7	0.8	0.8	0.9	1.0	1.1	1.2	1.2	10
12	0.1	0.2	0.3	0.4	0.5	0.6	0.7	0.8	0.9	1.0	1.1	1.2	1.3	1.4	1.5	12
14	0.1	0.2	0.4	0.5	0.6	0.7	0.8	0.9	1.0	1.2	1.3	1.4	1.5	1.6	1.8	14
16	0.1	0.3	0.4	0.5	0.7	0.8	0.9	1.1	1.2	1.3	1.5	1.6	1.7	1.9	2.0	16
18	0.2	0.3	0.4	0.6	0.8	0.9	1.0	1.2	1.4	1.5	1.6	1.8	2.0	2.1	2.2	18
20	0.2	0.3	0.5	0.7	0.8	1.0	1.2	1.3	1.5	1.7	1.8	2.0	2.2	2.3	2.5	20
22	0.2	0.4	0.6	0.7	0.9	1.1	1.3	1.5	1.6	1.8	2.0	2.2	2.4	2.6	2.8	22
24	0.2	0.4	0.6	0.8	1.0	1.2	1.4	1.6	1.8	2.0	2.2	2.4	2.6	2.8	3.0	24
26	0.2	0.4	0.6	0.9	1.1	1.3	1.5	1.7	2.0	2.2	2.4	2.6	2.8	3.0	3.2	26
28	0.2	0.5	0.7	0.9	1.2	1.4	1.6	1.9	2.1	2.3	2.6	2.8	3.0	3.3	3.5	28
30	0.2	0.5	0.8	1.0	1.2	1.5	1.8	2.0	2.2	2.5	2.8	3.0	3.3	3.5	3.8	30
32	0.3	0.5	0.8	1.1	1.3	1.6	1.9	2.1	2.4	2.7	2.9	3.2	3.5	3.7	4.0	32
34	0.3	0.6	0.8	1.1	1.4	1.7	2.0	2.3	2.6	2.8	3.1	3.4	3.7	4.0	4.2	34
36	0.3	0.6	0.9	1.2	1.5	1.8	2.1	2.4	2.7	3.0	3.3	3.6	3.9	4.2	4.5	36
38	0.3	0.6	1.0	1.3	1.6	1.9	2.2	2.5	2.8	3.2	3.5	3.8	4.1	4.4	4.8	38
40	0.3	0.7	1.0	1.3	1.7	2.0	2.3	2.7	3.0	3.3	3.7	4.0	4.3	4.7	5.0	40
42	0.4	0.7	1.0	1.4	1.8	2.1	2.4	2.8	3.2	3.5	3.8	4.2	4.6	4.9	5.2	42
44	0.4	0.7	1.1	1.5	1.8	2.2	2.6	2.9	3.3	3.7	4.0	4.4	4.8	5.1	5.5	44
46	0.4	0.8	1.2	1.5	1.9	2.3	2.7	3.1	3.4	3.8	4.2	4.6	5.0	5.4	5.8	46
48	0.4	0.8	1.2	1.6	2.0	2.4	2.8	3.2	3.6	4.0	4.4	4.8	5.2	5.6	6.0	48
50	0.4	0.8	1.2	1.7	2.1	2.5	2.9	3.3	3.8	4.2	4.6	5.0	5.4	5.8	6.2	50
52	0.4	0.9	1.3	1.7	2.2	2.6	3.0	3.5	3.9	4.3	4.8	5.2	5.6	6.1	6.5	52
54	0.4	0.9	1.4	1.8	2.2	2.7	3.2	3.6	4.0	4.5	5.0	5.4	5.8	6.3	6.8	54
56	0.5	0.9	1.4	1.9	2.3	2.8	3.3	3.7	4.2	4.7	5.1	5.6	6.1	6.5	7.0	56
58	0.5	1.0	1.4	1.9	2.4	2.9	3.4	3.9	4.4	4.8	5.3	5.8	6.3	6.8	7.2	58
60	0.5	1.0	1.5	2.0	2.5	3.0	3.5	4.0	4.5	5.0	5.5	6.0	6.5	7.0	7.5	60

Min.	Speed in Knots/MPH													Min.
	8.0	8.5	9.0	9.5	10.0	10.5	11.0	11.5	12.0	12.5	13.0	13.5	14.0	
	Distance in Nautical/Statute Miles													
2	0.3	0.3	0.3	0.3	0.3	0.4	0.4	0.4	0.4	0.4	0.4	0.4	0.5	2
4	0.5	0.6	0.6	0.6	0.7	0.7	0.7	0.8	0.8	0.8	0.9	0.9	0.9	4
6	0.8	0.8	0.9	1.0	1.0	1.0	1.1	1.2	1.2	1.2	1.3	1.4	1.4	6
8	1.1	1.1	1.2	1.3	1.3	1.4	1.5	1.5	1.6	1.7	1.7	1.8	1.9	8
10	1.3	1.4	1.5	1.6	1.7	1.8	1.8	1.9	2.0	2.1	2.2	2.2	2.3	10
12	1.6	1.7	1.8	1.9	2.0	2.1	2.2	2.3	2.4	2.5	2.6	2.7	2.8	12
14	1.9	2.0	2.1	2.2	2.3	2.4	2.6	2.7	2.8	2.9	3.0	3.3	3.3	14
16	2.1	2.3	2.4	2.5	2.7	2.8	2.9	3.1	3.2	3.3	3.5	3.6	3.7	16
18	2.4	2.6	2.7	2.8	3.0	3.2	3.3	3.4	3.6	3.8	3.9	4.0	4.2	18
20	2.7	2.8	3.0	3.2	3.3	3.5	3.7	3.8	4.0	4.2	4.3	4.5	4.7	20
22	2.9	3.1	3.3	3.5	3.7	3.8	4.0	4.2	4.4	4.6	4.8	5.0	5.1	22
24	3.2	3.4	3.6	3.8	4.0	4.2	4.4	4.6	4.8	5.0	5.2	5.4	5.6	24
26	3.5	3.7	3.9	4.1	4.3	4.6	4.8	5.0	5.2	5.4	5.6	5.8	6.1	26
28	3.7	4.0	4.2	4.4	4.7	4.9	5.1	5.4	5.6	5.8	6.1	6.3	6.5	28
30	4.0	4.2	4.5	4.8	5.0	5.2	5.5	5.8	6.0	6.2	6.5	6.8	7.0	30

Continued

Min.	\multicolumn{13}{c}{Speed in Knots/MPH}	Min.
	8.0	8.5	9.0	9.5	10.0	10.5	11.0	11.5	12.0	12.5	13.0	13.5	14.0	
	\multicolumn{13}{c}{Distance in Nautical/Statute Miles}	
32	4.3	4.5	4.8	5.1	5.3	5.6	5.9	6.1	6.4	6.7	6.9	7.2	7.5	32
34	4.5	4.8	5.1	5.4	5.7	6.0	6.2	6.5	6.8	7.1	7.4	7.6	7.9	34
36	4.8	5.1	5.4	5.7	6.0	6.3	6.6	6.9	7.2	7.5	7.8	8.1	8.4	36
38	5.1	5.4	5.7	6.0	6.3	6.6	7.0	7.3	7.6	7.9	8.2	8.6	8.9	38
40	5.3	5.7	6.0	6.3	6.7	7.0	7.3	7.7	8.0	8.3	8.7	9.0	9.3	40
42	5.6	6.0	6.3	6.6	7.0	7.4	7.7	8.0	8.4	8.8	9.1	9.4	9.8	42
44	5.9	6.2	6.6	7.0	7.3	7.7	8.1	8.4	8.8	9.2	9.5	9.9	10.3	44
46	6.1	6.5	6.9	7.3	7.7	8.0	8.4	8.8	9.2	9.6	10.0	10.4	10.7	46
48	6.4	6.8	7.2	7.6	8.0	8.4	8.8	9.2	9.6	10.0	10.4	10.8	11.2	48
50	6.7	7.1	7.5	7.9	8.3	8.8	9.2	9.6	10.0	10.4	10.8	11.2	11.7	50
52	6.9	7.4	7.8	8.2	8.7	9.1	9.5	10.0	10.4	10.8	11.3	11.7	12.1	52
54	7.2	7.6	8.1	8.6	9.0	9.4	9.9	10.4	10.8	11.2	11.7	12.2	12.6	54
56	7.5	7.9	8.4	8.9	9.3	9.8	10.3	10.7	11.2	11.7	12.1	12.6	13.1	56
58	7.7	8.2	8.7	9.2	9.7	10.2	10.6	11.1	11.6	12.1	12.6	13.0	13.5	58
60	8.0	8.5	9.0	9.5	10.0	10.5	11.0	11.5	12.0	12.5	13.0	13.5	14.0	60

Min.	\multicolumn{13}{c}{Speed in Knots/MPH}	Min.
	14.5	15.0	15.5	16.0	16.5	17.0	17.5	18.0	18.5	19.0	19.5	20.0		
	\multicolumn{13}{c}{Distance in Nautical/Statute Miles}	
2	0.5	0.5	0.5	0.5	0.6	0.6	0.6	0.6	0.6	0.6	0.6	0.7	2
4	1.0	1.0	1.0	1.0	1.1	1.1	1.2	1.2	1.2	1.3	1.3	1.3	4
6	1.4	1.5	1.6	1.6	1.6	1.7	1.8	1.8	1.8	1.9	2.0	2.0	6
8	1.9	2.0	2.1	2.1	2.2	2.3	2.3	2.4	2.5	2.5	2.6	2.7	8
10	2.4	2.5	2.6	2.7	2.8	2.8	2.9	3.0	3.1	3.2	3.2	3.3	10
12	2.9	3.0	3.1	3.2	3.3	3.4	3.5	3.6	3.7	3.8	3.9	4.0	12
14	3.4	3.5	3.6	3.7	3.8	4.0	4.1	4.2	4.3	4.4	4.6	4.7	14
16	3.9	4.0	4.1	4.3	4.4	4.5	4.7	4.8	4.9	5.1	5.2	5.3	16
18	4.4	4.5	4.6	4.8	5.0	5.1	5.2	5.4	5.6	5.7	5.8	6.0	18
20	4.8	5.0	5.2	5.3	5.5	5.7	5.8	6.0	6.2	6.3	6.5	6.7	20
22	5.3	5.5	5.7	5.9	6.0	6.2	6.4	6.6	6.8	7.0	7.2	7.3	22
24	5.8	6.0	6.2	6.4	6.6	6.8	7.0	7.2	7.4	7.6	7.8	8.0	24
26	6.3	6.5	6.7	6.9	7.2	7.4	7.6	7.8	8.0	8.2	8.4	8.7	26
28	6.8	7.0	7.2	7.5	7.7	7.9	8.2	8.4	8.6	8.9	9.1	9.3	28
30	7.2	7.5	7.8	8.0	8.2	8.5	8.8	9.0	9.2	9.5	9.8	10.0	30
32	7.7	8.0	8.3	8.5	8.8	9.1	9.3	9.6	9.9	10.1	10.4	10.7	32
34	8.2	8.5	8.8	9.1	9.4	9.6	9.9	10.2	10.5	10.8	11.0	11.3	34
36	8.7	9.0	9.3	9.6	9.9	10.2	10.5	10.8	11.1	11.4	11.7	12.0	36
38	9.2	9.5	9.8	10.1	10.4	10.8	11.1	11.4	11.7	12.0	12.4	12.7	38
40	9.7	10.0	10.3	10.7	11.0	11.3	11.7	12.0	12.3	12.7	13.0	13.3	40
42	10.2	10.5	10.8	11.2	11.6	11.9	12.2	12.6	13.0	13.3	13.6	14.0	42
44	10.6	11.0	11.4	11.7	12.1	12.5	12.8	13.2	13.6	13.9	14.3	14.7	44
46	11.1	11.5	11.9	12.3	12.6	13.0	13.4	13.8	14.2	14.6	15.0	15.3	46
48	11.6	12.0	12.4	12.8	13.2	13.6	14.0	14.4	14.8	15.2	15.6	16.0	48
50	12.1	12.5	12.9	13.3	13.8	14.2	14.6	15.0	15.4	15.8	16.2	16.7	50
52	12.6	13.0	13.4	13.9	14.3	14.7	15.2	15.6	16.0	16.5	16.9	17.3	52
54	13.0	13.5	14.0	14.4	14.8	15.3	15.8	16.2	16.6	17.1	17.6	18.0	54
56	13.5	14.0	14.5	14.9	15.1	15.6	16.0	16.5	17.0	17.4	17.9	18.3	56
58	14.0	14.5	15.0	15.5	16.0	16.4	16.9	17.4	17.9	18.4	18.8	19.3	58
60	14.5	15.0	15.5	16.0	16.5	17.0	17.5	18.0	18.5	19.0	19.5	20.0	60

Similarly, to find the distance run when you know your speed over the ground and elapsed time, enter the table on either the horizontal or the vertical axis, and the distance will be at the intersection of the speed and time columns. The table will work equally well to determine distances in units of statute miles and speeds in miles per hour, but the appropriate terms must be used throughout. That is, if you enter the table with distance run in nautical miles, then the speed will have to be in knots; conversely, if you use statute miles, you must also use statute miles per hour.

TABLE XII. CONVERSION TABLE: NAUTICAL/STATUTE MILES

To find kilometers, multiply statute miles x 1.6 or nautical miles x 1.85.

Nautical	Statute	Nautical	Statute	Statute	Nautical	Statute	Nautical
1.00	1.15	12.75	14.68	1.00	0.87	12.75	11.08
1.25	1.44	13.00	14.96	1.25	1.09	13.00	11.30
1.50	1.73	13.25	15.25	1.50	1.30	13.25	11.51
1.75	2.01	13.50	15.54	1.75	1.52	13.50	11.73
2.00	2.30	13.75	15.83	2.00	1.74	13.75	11.95
2.25	2.59	14.00	16.11	2.25	1.95	14.00	12.16
2.50	2.88	14.25	16.40	2.50	2.17	14.25	12.38
2.75	3.16	14.50	16.69	2.75	2.39	14.50	12.60
3.00	3.45	14.75	16.98	3.00	2.61	14.75	12.82
3.25	3.74			3.25	2.82		
3.50	4.03	15.00	17.27	3.50	3.04	15.00	13.03
3.75	4.32	15.25	17.55	3.75	3.26	15.25	13.25
4.00	4.60	15.50	17.84	4.00	3.47	15.50	13.47
4.25	4.89	15.75	18.13	4.25	3.69	15.75	13.69
4.50	5.18	16.00	18.42	4.50	3.91	16.00	13.90
4.75	5.47	16.25	18.70	4.75	4.13	16.25	14.12
		16.50	18.99			16.50	14.34
5.00	5.75	16.75	19.28	5.00	4.34	16.75	14.55
5.25	6.04	17.00	19.57	5.25	4.56	17.00	14.77
5.50	6.33	17.25	19.85	5.50	4.78	17.25	14.99
5.75	6.62	17.50	20.15	5.75	5.00	17.50	15.21
6.00	6.91	17.75	20.43	6.00	5.21	17.75	15.42
6.25	7.19	18.00	20.72	6.25	5.43	18.00	15.64
6.50	7.48	18.25	21.01	6.50	5.65	18.25	15.86
6.75	7.77	18.50	21.29	6.75	5.86	18.50	16.08
7.00	8.06	18.75	21.58	7.00	6.08	18.75	16.29
7.25	8.34	19.00	21.87	7.25	6.30	19.00	16.51
7.50	8.63	19.25	22.16	7.50	6.52	19.25	16.73
7.75	8.92	19.50	22.44	7.75	6.73	19.50	16.94
8.00	9.21	19.75	22.73	8.00	6.95	19.75	17.16
8.25	9.50			8.25	7.17		
8.50	9.78	20.00	23.02	8.50	7.39	20.00	17.38
8.75	10.07	20.25	23.31	8.75	7.60	20.25	17.60
9.00	10.36	20.50	23.60	9.00	7.82	20.50	17.81
9.25	10.65	20.75	23.88	9.25	8.04	20.75	18.03
9.50	10.93	21.00	24.17	9.50	8.25	21.00	18.25
9.75	11.22	21.25	24.46	9.75	8.47	21.25	18.46
		21.50	24.75			21.50	18.68
10.00	11.51	21.75	25.03	10.00	8.69	21.75	18.90
10.25	11.80	22.00	25.32	10.25	8.91	22.00	19.12
10.50	12.09	22.25	25.61	10.50	9.12	22.25	19.33
10.75	12.37	22.50	25.90	10.75	9.34	22.50	19.55
11.00	12.66	22.75	26.19	11.00	9.56	22.75	19.77
11.25	12.95	23.00	26.47	11.25	9.77	23.00	19.99
11.50	13.24	23.50	27.05	11.50	9.99	23.25	20.20
11.75	13.52	24.00	27.62	11.75	10.21	23.50	20.42
12.00	13.81	24.50	28.20	12.00	10.43	23.75	20.64
12.25	14.10	25.00	28.78	12.25	10.64	24.00	20.85
12.50	14.39			12.50	10.86	24.50	21.29
						25.00	21.72

Tacking Extra Distance

Current aside, a skipper may sail a course that's not a straight line to his destination, either from convenience or necessity: tacking upwind is one such instance, and tacking downwind, as many cruising boats do, is another. The table below gives the extra distance sailed for selected angles by which a boat's headings might deviate from a straight-line course.

Angle	% Extra		Angle	% Extra
0°	0		25°	10%
5°	0.4%		30°	15%
10°	1.5%		35°	22%
15°	3.5%		40°	31%
20°	6.4%		45°	41%

Distance Covered at a Steady Speed

Table XIII shows the distances covered by a ship traveling at fixed speeds over ground for various periods of time. Obviously, if the unit of speed used when entering the left-hand column is knots, the distance covered will be in nautical miles per hour; if the unit of speed is statute miles per hour, the distance traveled will be in statute miles.

TABLE XIII. DISTANCES COVERED IN VARIOUS TIMES AT FIXED SPEEDS

Knots/ MPH	Distance Covered (Nautical/Statute Miles) In					
	6 hr	8 hr	12 hr	24 hr	48 hr	week
3	18	24	36	72	144	504
3.5	21	28	42	84	168	588
4	24	32	48	96	192	672
4.5	27	36	54	108	216	756
5	30	40	60	120	240	840
5.5	33	44	66	132	264	924
6	36	48	72	144	288	1008
6.5	39	52	78	156	312	1092
7	42	56	84	168	336	1176
7.5	45	60	90	180	360	1260
8	48	64	96	192	384	1344
8.5	51	68	102	204	408	1428
9	54	72	108	216	432	1512
9.5	57	76	114	228	456	1595
10	60	80	120	240	480	1680
10.5	63	84	126	252	504	1764
11	66	88	132	264	528	1848
11.5	69	92	138	276	552	1932
12	72	96	144	288	576	2016
12.5	75	100	150	300	600	2100
13	78	104	156	312	624	2184
13.5	81	108	162	324	648	2268
14	84	112	168	336	672	2352
14.5	87	116	174	348	696	2436

Continued

Knots/ MPH	Distance Covered (Nautical/Statute Miles) In					
	6 hr	8 hr	12 hr	24 hr	48 hr	week
15	90	120	180	360	720	2520
15.5	93	124	186	372	744	2604
16	96	128	192	384	768	2688
16.5	99	132	198	396	792	2772
17	102	136	204	408	816	2856
17.5	105	140	210	420	840	2940
18	108	144	216	432	864	3024
18.5	111	148	222	444	888	3108
19	114	152	228	456	912	3192
19.5	117	156	234	468	936	3276
20	120	160	240	480	960	3360

DUTCHMAN'S LOG

While instruments have refined the accuracy of speed/time/distance calculation, the wary navigator never depends wholly on mechanical contrivances, which tend to operate according to Murphy's Law: "If something can go wrong, it will, usually at the most inconvenient time."

Following is an elementary method for determining speed through the water with no instruments except a stopwatch. In the absence of a reliable watch, a simple verbal count of seconds (such as counting aloud, "one thousand-one, one thousand-two, one thousand-three. . .") will work well enough (it wouldn't hurt to practice periodically against a timer).

By noting the time required for the boat to pass an object — fixed, or floating but stationary — close alongside, the boat's speed can easily be determined once the following table has been completed. To complete the table, multiply the boat's overall length in feet by 3,600 (the number of seconds in one hour). Divide the result by 6,080 (for speeds in knots) or 5,280 (for speeds in statute miles). The answer is the speed in knots or miles per hour for a passing interval of one second. By dividing this answer by two, three, four, and so on, a matching speed for each of these passing intervals can be obtained and entered below.

Example: A boat is 30 feet overall. For a passing interval of one second,
$$\frac{30 \times 3600}{6080} = 17.8 \text{ knots}.$$

Time interval of two seconds = 8.9 knots.
Time interval of three seconds = 5.9 knots.

The system as described requires two people in addition to the helmsman — one at the bow and one at the stern. For shorthanded vessels, it may be simpler to inscribe sighting lines abreast of the helmsman's position, and use the distance from these forward to the bow as the boat's effective length in the table opposite.

In the absence of convenient markers, a floating object — preferably something that can be eaten by gulls or fish, but at least something biodegradable — can be thrown over the side.

Passing Interval (Seconds)	Speed	
	Knots	MPH
1	_____	
2	_____	
3	_____	
4	_____	
5	_____	
6	_____	
7	_____	
8	_____	
9	_____	
10	_____	

CONSTRUCTING A SPEED CURVE

A speed curve is a graphic representation of a boat's range of speeds through the water at various throttle settings. To be accurate, it requires an engine equipped with a tachometer. Besides giving a good idea of boat speed at all throttle settings from dead slow to full speed, a speed curve can also indicate the best cruising speed — the point beyond which more r.p.m. produce only minimal added speed; although this should indicate the hull speed of a displacement craft, it may be considerably below hull speed in some vessels.

To construct a speed curve using the following graph, locate a measured nautical mile or half-mile in your area. At successive tachometer settings, each separated by an interval width approximately equal to 10% of the maximum r.p.m., make a series of timed runs (one in each direction for each throttle setting).

Calculate and then average the paired speeds, and enter the result of each at the appropriate point on the graph. Connect the points, and you have your speed curve.

Remember, when making the timed runs, to load the boat to normal cruising trim and fill the tanks half-full. Using the speed curve should give good results as long as the boat's bottom surfaces remain relatively unchanged, and when load, wind, and sea conditions are approximately the same. When using the speed curve in coastal navigation, bear in mind that it does not take into account current or leeway.

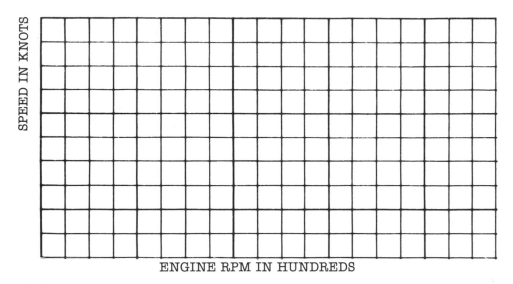

SPEED IN KNOTS (vertical axis label)

ENGINE RPM IN HUNDREDS

TABLE XIV. SPEED OVER A MEASURED MILE

If a nautical mile, boat's speed is in knots; if a statute mile, boat's speed is in statute miles per hour.

| Seconds | Minutes | | | | | | | | | | |
	3	4	5	6	7	8	9	10	11	12	13
0	20.00	15.00	12.00	10.00	8.57	7.50	6.67	·6.00	5.46	5.00	4.61
2	19.78	14.88	11.92	9.95	8.53	7.47	6.64	5.98	5.44	4.99	4.60
4	19.56	14.75	11.84	9.89	8.49	7.44	6.62	5.96	5.42	4.97	4.59
6	19.36	14.63	11.76	9.84	8.45	7.41	6.59	5.94	5.40	4.96	4.58
8	19.15	14.52	11.69	9.78	8.41	7.38	6.57	5.92	5.39	4.94	4.57
10	18.95	14.40	11.61	9.73	8.37	7.35	6.54	5.90	5.37	4.93	4.56
12	18.75	14.29	11.54	9.68	8.33	7.32	6.52	5.88	5.36	4.92	4.55
14	18.56	14.17	11.46	9.63	8.30	7.29	6.50	5.86	5.34	4.90	4.54
16	18.37	14.06	11.39	9.57	8.26	7.26	6.48	5.84	5.32	4.89	4.53
18	18.18	13.95	11.32	9.52	8.22	7.23	6.45	5.82	5.31	4.88	4.52
20	18.00	13.85	11.25	9.47	8.18	7.20	6.43	5.81	5.29	4.86	4.51
22	17.82	13.74	11.18	9.42	8.14	7.17	6.41	5.79	5.28	4.85	4.50
24	17.65	13.64	11.11	9.38	8.11	7.14	6.38	5.77	5.26	4.84	4.49
26	17.47	13.53	11.04	9.33	8.07	7.12	6.36	5.75	5.25	4.83	4.48
28	17.31	13.43	10.98	9.28	8.04	7.09	6.34	5.73	5.23	4.81	4.47
30	17.14	13.33	10.91	9.23	8.00	7.06	6.32	5.71	5.22	4.80	4.46
32	16.98	13.24	10.84	9.18	7.96	7.03	6.29	5.70	5.20	4.79	4.45
34	16.82	13.14	10.78	9.14	7.93	7.00	6.27	5.68	5.19	4.78	4.44
36	16.68	13.04	10.71	9.09	7.90	6.98	6.25	5.66	5.17	4.76	4.43
38	16.51	12.95	10.65	9.04	7.86	6.95	6.23	5.64	5.16	4.75	4.42
40	16.36	12.86	10.59	9.00	7.83	6.92	6.21	5.62	5.14	4.74	4.41
42	16.22	12.77	10.53	8.96	7.79	6.90	6.19	5.61	5.13	4.72	4.40
44	16.07	12.68	10.46	8.91	7.76	6.87	6.16	5.59	5.11	4.71	4.39
46	15.93	12.59	10.40	8.87	7.72	6.84	6.14	5.57	5.10	4.70	4.38
48	15.79	12.50	10.34	8.82	7.69	6.82	6.12	5.56	5.08	4.69	4.37
50	15.65	12.41	10.29	8.78	7.66	6.79	6.10	5.54	5.07	4.68	4.36
52	15.52	12.33	10.23	8.74	7.63	6.77	6.08	5.52	5.06	4.66	4.35
54	15.38	12.24	10.17	8.70	7.60	6.74	6.06	5.50	5.04	4.65	4.34
56	15.25	12.16	10.11	8.65	7.56	6.72	6.04	5.49	5.03	4.64	4.33
58	15.13	12.08	10.06	8.61	7.53	6.69	6.02	5.47	5.01	4.63	4.32
60	15.00	12.00	10.00	8.57	7.50	6.67	6.00	5.46	5.00	4.61	4.31

Continued

		Minutes					
		14	15	16	17	18	19
Seconds	0	4.3	4.0	3.8	3.5	3.3	3.2
	15	4.2	3.9	3.7	3.5	3.3	3.1
	30	4.1	3.9	3.6	3.4	3.2	3.1
	45	4.1	3.8	3.6	3.4	3.2	3.0
	60	4.0	3.8	3.5	3.3	3.2	3.0

SPEED, FUEL CONSUMPTION, RANGE: PERSONAL BOAT DATA

The table below allows you to keep a record of your boat's speeds through calm water, at various throttle settings. You will need a measured-mile course — usually available locally — and the tables in this chapter. For best results, it is customary to load the boat with her normal complement of gear and have her fuel tanks half-full. The mile should be run once in each direction for each throttle setting, and the average of the two speeds noted in the tachometer table below. (If you have completed the speed curve in the previous section, you have already gone through this procedure.)

For those boats, including most outboards, that have very elementary throttle arrangements, it is sufficient to note the speeds associated with named throttle settings, such as **Slow, Start,** and **Fast.**

It's a good idea to check at least the three principal throttle settings and related speeds about once a month, as the seasonal accumulation of marine growth can substantially cut a boat's early-summer calculated speeds.

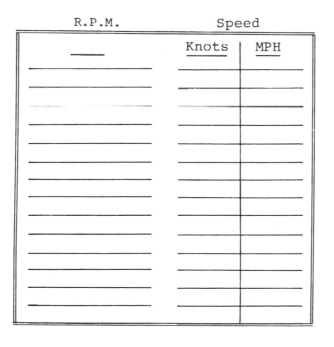

If you have the time and the inclination, you may want to determine the boat's fuel consumption at various settings; then, combining that data with the information from the preceding table, complete the following table for a record of maximum ranges at the designated throttle settings.

FUEL CONSUMPTION - RANGE

THROTTLE	GALLONS per hour	SPEED		RANGE IN HOURS	RANGE IN MILES	
		Knots	MPH		Nautical	Statute
SLOW						
CRUISING						
MAX. CONTINUOUS						

3/ DIRECTION

If there is only one instrument on your boat, it should almost certainly be a good marine compass. The problem, of course, is that good ones are very expensive — and seem more so, for they are small and deceptively simple to look at. Several authorities hold that you should figure out the most that you can afford for a compass, then buy one a bit more expensive than that. This seems to me fairly silly, since a relatively low-cost compass may be quite adequate for the kind of piloting you are going to do. My own prescription, then, is to decide what you want the instrument to do: will 5° intervals be close enough? Is sailboat gimbaling necessary? Will you need self-contained lighting? Flush or bracket mounting? Having made your decisions, then buy the best compass you can within those parameters.

The details of compass installation are covered later in this chapter. Before mounting your compass permanently, check to see that your location will have as many as possible of the following assets:

1. Good view of the lubber's line from the helmsman's position; some sailboat compasses provide auxiliary vanes for secondary lubber's lines at 45° to the primary line, as a sighting aid for the tiller-wielding skipper.
2. A location suitable for taking bearings without removing the compass from its binnacle or mounting. Full 360° visibility at and slightly above the horizon line is best, but 100° aft from the ship's heading on either side is probably adequate.
3. No potential nearby sources of magnetic deviation. If this isn't possible, try to site the compass away from frequently used electrical gadgets, like windshield wipers.

A compass with a built-in angle of heel indicator is useful (if hardly vital) on most sailboats. And even if your compass' location is excellent for taking bearings, it's a fine idea to have aboard an inexpensive hand-bearing compass. Not only will such an instrument enable you to take bearings without disturbing the man at the wheel, it will also serve as a substitute if the steering compass is lost or damaged. In this connection, it doesn't hurt to prepare in advance a suitable mounting and its associated deviation table, appropriate for use of the bearing compass for steering. Needless to say, you won't try to compensate a non-mounted hand-bearing compass. Also needless (I hope) to say, you won't try to use an undamped, hiker's compass with a free-swinging needle.

Today's lightweight, compact radio direction finders (RDF) are so useful that they can rank above most other devices (depth sounder perhaps excepted) as the next instrument to buy. If you can, get one that has all the bands, from beacon up through the top end of the medium-frequency marine band. Other assets are dual power supply (ship's and self-contained), visual null meter, beat frequency oscillator and sense antenna (to eliminate 180° ambiguity), and provision for permanent mounting.

COMPASS POINTS AND DEGREES

Although the vast majority of pleasure boatmen use the 360-degree system for designating directions, they are only kidding themselves a good deal of the time. The average yacht helmsman is doing well to hold his boat within two or three degrees on either side of the nominal course. The ancient point method, in which the 360 degrees of the full circle were described by 128 points, may have been more functionally accurate, in that the divisions between points — 2¾ degrees — were more realistic.

Few compasses are seen today with cards divided into the point system, and probably the old arrangement is just too much trouble to learn, as well as being far too much trouble to work with. Still, I have found it useful, in a modified form, especially when talking about general tendencies — wind direction, or course made good over a day at sea. Somehow, a course or direction of NNE is more meaningful to me than 022°.

TABLE XV. COMPASS POINTS

FIRST QUARTER		SECOND QUARTER	
Points	Degrees	Points	Degrees
North	0	East	90
N 1/4 E	2 3/4	E 1/4 S	92 3/4
N 1/2 E	5 1/2	E 1/2 S	95 1/2
N 3/4 E	8 1/2	E 3/4 S	98 1/2
N by E	11 1/4	E by S	101 1/4
N by E 1/4 E	14	E by S 1/4 S	104
N by E 1/2 E	17	E by S 1/2 S	107
N by E 3/4 E	19 3/4	E by S 3/4 S	109 3/4
NNE	22 1/2	ESE	112 1/2
NE by N 3/4 N	25 1/4	SE by E 3/4 E	115 1/4
NE by N 1/2 N	28	SE by E 1/2 E	118
NE by N 1/4 N	31	SE by E 1/4 E	121
NE by N	33 3/4	SE by E	123 3/4
NE 3/4 N	36 1/2	SE 3/4 E	126 1/2
NE 1/2 N	39 1/4	SE 1/2 E	129 1/4
NE 1/4 N	42 1/4	SE 1/4 E	132 1/4
NE	45	SE	135
NE 1/4 E	47 3/4	SE 1/4 S	137 3/4
NE 1/2 E	50 1/2	SE 1/2 S	140 1/2
NE 3/4 E	53 1/2	SE 3/4 S	143 1/2
NE by E	56 1/4	SE by S	146 1/4
NE by E 1/4 E	59	SE by S 1/4 S	149
NE by E 1/2 E	62	SE by S 1/2 S	152
NE by E 3/4 E	64 3/4	SE by S 3/4 S	154 3/4
ENE	67 1/2	SSE	157 1/2
E by N 3/4 N	70 1/4	S by E 3/4 E	160 1/4
E by N 1/2 N	73	S by E 1/2 E	163
E by N 1/4 N	76	S by E 1/4 E	166
E by N	78 3/4	S by E	168 3/4
E 3/4 N	81 1/2	S 3/4 E	171 1/2
E 1/2 N	84 1/4	S 1/2 E	174 1/4
E 1/4 N	87 1/4	S 1/4 E	177 1/4
East	90	South	180

THIRD QUARTER		FOURTH QUARTER	
Points	Degrees	Points	Degrees
South	180	West	270
S 1/4 W	182 3/4	W 1/4 N	272 3/4
S 1/2 W	185 1/2	W 1/2 N	275 1/2
S 3/4 W	188 1/2	W 3/4 N	278 1/2
S by W	191 1/4	W by N	281 1/4
S by W 1/4 W	194	W by N 1/4 N	284
S by W 1/2 W	197	W by N 1/2 N	287
S by W 3/4 W	199 3/4	W by N 3/4 N	289 3/4
SSW	202 1/2	WNW	292 1/2
SW by S 3/4 S	205 1/4	NW by W 3/4 W	295 1/4
SW by S 1/2 S	208	NW by W 1/2 W	298
SW by S 1/4 S	211	NW by W 1/4 W	301
SW by S	213 3/4	NW by W	303 3/4
SW 3/4 S	216 1/2	NW 3/4 W	306 1/2
SW 1/2 S	219 1/2	NW 1/2 W	309 1/2
SW 1/4 S	222 1/4	NW 1/4 W	312 1/4
SW	225	NW	315
SW 1/4 W	227 3/4	NW 1/4 N	317 3/4
SW 1/2 W	230 1/2	NW 1/2 N	320 1/2
SW 3/4 W	233 1/2	NW 3/4 N	323 1/2
SW by W	236 1/4	NW by N	326 1/4
SW by W 1/4 W	239	NW by N 1/4 N	329
SW by W 1/2 W	242	NW by N 1/2 N	332
SW by W 3/4 W	244 3/4	NW by N 3/4 N	334 3/4
WSW	247 1/2	NNW	337 1/2
W by S 3/4 S	250 1/4	N by W 3/4 W	340 1/4
W by S 1/2 S	253	N by W 1/2 W	343
W by S 1/4 S	256	N by W 1/4 W	346
W by S	258 3/4	N by W	348 3/4
W 3/4 S	261 1/2	N 3/4 W	351 1/2
W 1/2 S	264 1/4	N 1/2 W	354 1/4
W 1/4 S	267 1/4	N 1/4 W	357 1/4
West	270	North	360/000

COMPENSATING YOUR COMPASS

Nearly every good-quality marine compass can be compensated to eliminate or radically reduce its deviation. If deviation can be reduced to near-zero, it obviously simplifies the pilot's problem. Even with some deviation remaining in your compass, the instrument is still much more convenient for quick, offhand bearings if you can rely on its accuracy within five degrees or so.

A compass should be compensated when it is first installed aboard, and recompensated annually or each time the vessel has a major overhaul. Any replacement or relocation of equipment near the compass — especially electronic equipment — is probably cause for checking the compass' accuracy.

Step 1. Location: Check the area within which you plan to mount the compass for absence (when possible) of magnetic objects. If there are electrical switches or installations in the area, activate each one in turn with the compass in close proximity, and observe whether or not a change in compass deviation results. If the compass in its intended location can be easily viewed from the helmsman's station, and if sighting over the compass without removing it from its binnacle will be possible, then the location is probably good.

Step 2. Zeroing: Compasses with built-in compensators (internal, adjustable magnets) must be zeroed before final mounting. This simply ensures that the compass, prior to installation, is responding solely to the earth's field; any magnetic influences emanating from the vessel will then operate on the compass freely.

In an area clear of magnetic influences (probably ashore), mount the compass, using nonmagnetic screws, to a small, square board, in such a way that a line from the center of the compass card through the lubber's line is parallel to two edges of the board. Place the board on a flat surface and turn it until the compass points exactly North. Draw lines on the flat surface, along the two edges of the board that are parallel to the registered North-South axis. Now rotate the board and compass 180 degrees. If the compass reads exactly South, then its North-South alignment is correct. If not, turn the N-S adjusting screw (usually so marked), until **half** the error is removed, being careful to use a nonmagnetic screwdriver.

Reverse the board; if the compass needle does not now point North, halve the error again. Reverse the board yet another time, and halve the remaining error. Continue this procedure until the North-South alignment is correct. Now rotate the board 90 degrees and align the compass East and West, using the same procedure.

Step 3. Installation: Take the zeroed compass to the selected shipboard mounting site. Make sure that the compass' fore-and-aft axis is parallel to the vessel centerline (don't put too much faith in the exact athwartships alignment of the bulkheads). Mount the compass with nonmagnetic fastenings. Now activate by turn each electrical or electronic device anywhere near the compass. If the deviation is altered when any one of them is operating, and if it's not possible to relocate the compass, you'll need an additional deviation table to reflect the condition. First compensate the compass in the normal fashion, with the offending electrical device on or off (whichever is the more usual condition). After compensation, if there is still excessive deviation — more than two or three degrees — construct a deviation table that reflects the boat's electrical devices in their normal operating mode. Finally, construct a separate table to be used when the device causing the altered deviation is off or on (whichever is the **less** usual mode).

Step 4. Compensation: In most harbors, it should be possible to establish a set of ranges at approximate 15° intervals through 360°. Ranges need not consist solely of aids to navigation, and indeed the best range does not rely on buoys or other anchored aids. Each range, of course, contains its own reciprocal, although in the case of a range with one element on or near shore, a back bearing may be necessary. If possible, a pelorus should be employed to facilitate accuracy when establishing ranges.

Again, the only tool required is a nonmagnetic screwdriver. All gear should be stowed or arranged as it will be under normal operating conditions. If the compass has internal compensating magnets, proceed with compensation in exactly the same way as in Step 2 above. If no nearly exact N-S and E-W ranges can be found, a single marker may be used by steering first a course of 0° or 90°, then making a tight turn and steering 180° or 270°, respectively, for not less than half a mile. Compensation, like the process of zeroing-in, is based upon the assumption that equal and opposite deviation exists on reciprocal courses.

If external correcting magnets are used, the procedure is a bit more complicated. The steps to take are set out in **Chapman's Piloting, Seamanship and Small Boat Handling** — but there is really little need to buy a compass without self-contained compensators in the first place. Having corrected the four cardinal points, use the deviation table on page 43 for noting error on other headings.

To simplify annual compensation, use the following table to identify a complete set of ranges located in your harbor or nearby. Remember that a floating aid marking one end of a range should be checked to ensure that its position does not shift from one year to the next.

	Marks			Ranges (Magnetic)	
Front		Back	First		Reciprocal
————		————	————		————
————		————	————		————
————		————	————		————
————		————	————		————
————		————	————		————
————		————	————		————
————		————	————		————
————		————	————		————
————		————	————		————
————		————	————		————
————		————	————		————
————		————	————		————

Date last used:_____

Deviation Curve

If you cannot fully compensate your compass, or don't choose to, you'll need a deviation table. These can take several forms, but the tabular curve on page 43 has, I think, some significant advantages. To begin with, it is easy to use — easier for most people than the Napier diagram, the other common deviation curve. It is also easy to construct, especially if the pilot has the aid of a French curve, obtainable in most art supply stores at modest cost. Finally, the ranges employed need not be exact multiples of five or fifteen degrees: you can plot the ranges available, as long as they're approximately 15° apart.

In this table, the horizontal lines designate 15° increments for magnetic courses. The vertical lines refer to compass deviation, with deviations west and east located left and right, respectively, of the 0° line. If ranges exactly 15° apart aren't available, interpolation is quite accurate enough.

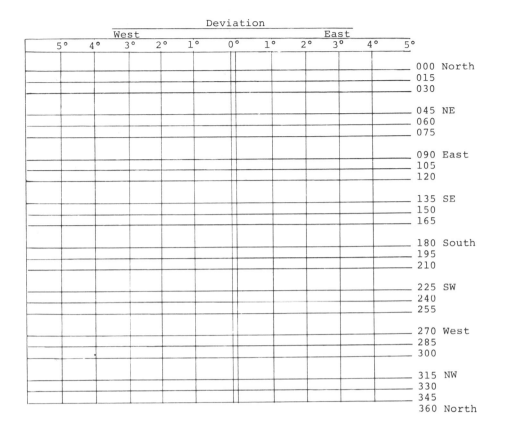

CORRECTING AND UNCORRECTING

Despite — or perhaps because of — all the mnemonics designed to help the navigator remember whether to add or subtract deviation and variation, I always forget. Even when I haven't forgotten, it worries me. Judging by my friends, "TVMDC" and "Subtract East–Add West" are nagging irritations to others, as well. There are two ways to banish these worries forever from your mind (short of actually learning the rules once and for all, that is): one is to compensate your compass fully (see the instructions in this chapter) to eliminate deviation, and buy a protractor — there are several brands — that converts between true and magnetic headings. If this procedure isn't practical for you, then consult Figure 5.

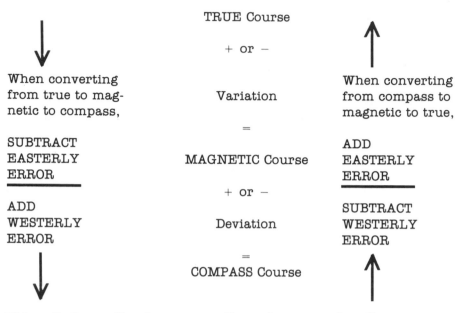

Figure 5. Converting true, magnetic, and compass headings

Most small craft skippers can forget about true courses, correcting only from magnetic to compass. But charted ranges are noted as true directions, so it's useful to be able to cope with the whole "TVMDC" progression when necessary.

When converting compass bearings to magnetic directions, remember to use the deviation that applies to the compass heading at the time of the bearing, not the deviation associated with the bearing itself. For example, if you take a compass bearing of 300° while on a compass heading of 180°, the deviation to be applied in converting from compass bearing to magnetic direction is that associated with 180°.

TILT CORRECTION

If your auxiliary sailing vessel has a binnacle compass mounted over the inboard engine, the compass deviation may be altered when the boat is heeled. Larger ships are equipped with a heeling magnet under the compass to compensate for this effect, but this usually involves the cost and difficulty of hiring a professional compass adjuster and arranging for the required angles of heel.

It's probably simpler to test the boat on a couple of local ranges by comparing the deviation at selected angles of heel to that noted on the standard deviation table. If a significant error turns up, the following table can be filled out for future reference.

44

Magnetic Heading	Angle of Heel			
	_____ °	_____ °	_____ °	_____ °
	Deviation at Selected Angle of Heel			
000	_____	_____	_____	_____
015	_____	_____	_____	_____
030	_____	_____	_____	_____
045	_____	_____	_____	_____
060	_____	_____	_____	_____
075	_____	_____	_____	_____
090	_____	_____	_____	_____
105	_____	_____	_____	_____
120	_____	_____	_____	_____
135	_____	_____	_____	_____
150	_____	_____	_____	_____
165	_____	_____	_____	_____
180	_____	_____	_____	_____
195	_____	_____	_____	_____
210	_____	_____	_____	_____
225	_____	_____	_____	_____
240	_____	_____	_____	_____
255	_____	_____	_____	_____
270	_____	_____	_____	_____
285	_____	_____	_____	_____
300	_____	_____	_____	_____
315	_____	_____	_____	_____
330	_____	_____	_____	_____
345	_____	_____	_____	_____
360	_____	_____	_____	_____

RDF DEVIATION TABLE

Like your ship's compass, your RDF can be affected by sources of deviation within the vessel (a frequent source is wire standing rigging). RDFs should be permanently or semipermanently located, and the following deviation table completed when an active radiobeacon is within sight of the boat.

This table should be compiled using the low-frequency marine radiobeacons in your area. It should then be checked against other useful transmitter types — airport radiobeacons, commercial stations — as the deviation may not be the same at higher frequencies. Another deviation curve in a different color may be overlaid on the low-frequency curve if necessary.

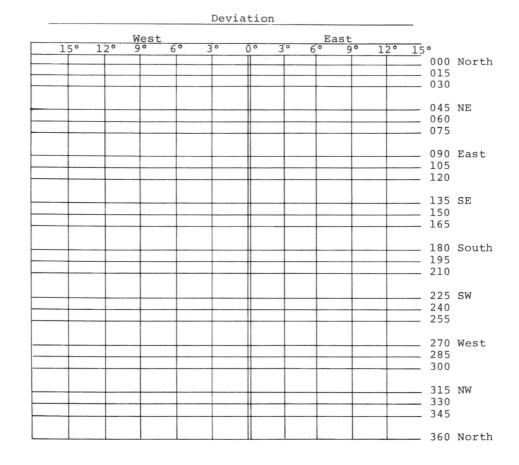

Marine Radiobeacons

Marine radiobeacons, which operate in the low-frequency band between 285 and 325 kHz, are of two types:

1. Low-power **marker beacons** have a nominal range of 10 or 20 miles; in many cases a direction-finding range of five miles will be more usual. These beacons transmit a continuous, omnidirectional signal consisting of two (or occasionally one) Morse code letters.

2. **Primary radiobeacons** have a nominal range of anywhere from 30 up to 100 or 125 miles. While the more high-powered beacons of this type can be heard at distances beyond their nominal range, it is usually impossible to employ them for direction finding until well inside that range. Primary beacons may transmit continuously; however, they are also found in groups of up to six beacons on the same frequency, transmitting in sequenced order. In the latter case, a single radiobeacon will transmit its one- or two-letter Morse code signal for 48 seconds, following which time there are two seconds of silence; finally, the radiobeacon emits a 10-second dash, which is of course the signal on which to zero in for direction finding. At the end of the 10-second dash, the next beacon in the sequence will commence its call.

Transmission Cycle of Sequenced Radiobeacon

seconds

```
0        10        20        30        40        50        60
┌────────────────────────────────────────────┬───┬──────────┐
│       ⎡ Radiobeacon:  characteristic ⎤      │   │    10    │
│  ←────⎢ identifying signal           ⎢────→ │   │  second  │
│       ⎣                              ⎦      │   │   dash   │
└────────────────────────────────────────────┴───┴──────────┘
```

The positional number of a beacon (from I to VI) within a sequence is given in the **Light List** compilation of radiobeacons, and in most other lists as well. Thus, if one has an accurate chronometer, one can use the following table to determine which minutes in each hour a given beacon of a sequence will transmit.

Group	Minutes of hour of transmission cycle									
I	0	6	12	18	24	30	36	42	48	54
II	1	7	13	19	25	31	37	43	49	55
III	2	8	14	20	26	32	38	44	50	56
IV	3	9	15	21	27	33	39	45	51	57
V	4	10	16	22	28	34	40	46	52	58
VI	5	11	17	23	29	35	41	47	53	59

Most primary radiobeacons use a Morse code identifier that is related to the beacon's name — **NS** for Nantucket Shoals Lightship, for instance, or **OA** for Oak Island Light. But this is not always true: Miami's 100-mile radiobeacon transmits the single-letter identifier **U**, and Ambrose Tower, the entrance beacon for New York Harbor, transmits **T**. The same holds true for marker beacons: Brenton Reef's 10-mile identifier is **BR,** but nearby Little Gull Island sends the single letter **J.**

Figure 6. Morse code

```
A . _        I . .          Q _ _ . _      Y _ . _ _
B _ . . .    J . _ _ _      R . _ .        Z _ _ . .
C _ . _ .    K _ . _        S . . .
D _ . .      L . _ . .      T _
E .          M _ _          U . . _
F . . _ .    N _ .          V . . . _
G _ _ .      O _ _ _        W . _ _
H . . . .    P . _ _ .      X _ . . _
```

Airport radiobeacons operate in the band (325-410 kHz) immediately above that used by marine beacons. If an aerobeacon's antenna is on or near the shore, it can be just as useful as a marine radiobeacon; locations of such aerobeacons are indicated on most marine charts. The

47

characteristic signal of an aerobeacon is continuous and consists of two or three Morse code letters; the signal may be interrupted for weather reports at 15 and 45 minutes past the hour.

LOCAL RADIOBEACON TABLE

Station name - Location	Group	Signal	Frequency	Range

4/ POSITION

A number of operations — and a number of tools — contribute to the determination of your boat's position. For most pilots, the compass is the single, all-important positioning tool, as important here as it is in determining direction. Every pilot's kit should contain at least one, and possibly two good pairs of nonrusting dividers. A stopwatch is perhaps not a necessity, but it's a great advance beyond even the best sweep-second-hand wristwatch. In a real pinch, you can count short periods (as in timing a light) with surprising accuracy, by counting "one thousand-one, one thousand-two, one thousand-three," and so on. It helps to time yourself against a stopwatch until you have the rhythm right.

There are so many brands and styles of course protractors that it's really impossible to pick out a single "best" one. My own favorite for many years was a plastic device with a swing arm, into which you could crank the variation before setting the course. Any parallel or meridian gave you the single reference line required. It may be far more sporting, however, to work with a set of old-fashioned parallel rulers, or a pair of triangles. It depends on what you want.

For taking and plotting serious bearings, a good, handy, hand-bearing compass is a great addition, as is a three-arm protractor. The new, cheap, plastic sextants, which cost $50 to $125, now bring this tool within everyone's reach. These sextants seem to work quite well, especially for the relatively gross angles involved in coastal navigation.

The tables and methods in this section represent a fairly comprehensive collection of the many ways of establishing one's position. Many of them will be familiar to you, some of them won't. When the chance offers itself,

49

try your hand at one of the unfamiliar systems. You might find it a valuable and interesting new technique.

DISTANCE FINDING BY SOUND

At average summer temperatures, sound travels according to the following table (distances are nautical miles).

Distance (Miles)	Time (Seconds)	Distance (Miles)	Time (Seconds)
0.2	1	2.25	12.5
0.4	2	2.5	14
0.6	3	2.75	15
1.0	5.5	3.0	16.5
1.25	7	3.25	18
1.5	8	3.5	19
1.75	9.5	3.75	20.5
2.0	11	4.0	22

Sound speeds vary with the temperature, although not greatly. At 40 degrees Fahrenheit, the speed of sound is 1,100 feet per second, or 4.8 seconds per statute mile (5.5 seconds per nautical mile). At 70°F., sound travels 1,130 feet per second, and at 90°F., its speed is 1,150 feet per second, or 4.6 seconds per statute mile (about 760 statute m.p.h.).

It is possible to navigate by echo, especially in waters that are constricted by steeply sloping land masses. A sharp, relatively high-pitched sound creates the best echo; unfortunately, most of the freon-powered hand horns (which give a suitable noise) cannot be controlled as precisely as an electric horn. Based on a speed of 1,100 feet per second, a sound will travel about 0.2 mile per second. In estimating distance off by means of a self-produced sound, the pilot must remember to **double** the times in the table above, since the sound has to go two ways. A rough approximation can be arrived at by allowing 10 seconds per mile.

Precise echoes usually indicate a relatively tall, hard surface that is more or less vertical. Since fog not only muffles sounds but also distorts the direction from which they come, any type of sound navigation in fog, except distance finding, is erratic.

50

USE OF THE SEXTANT IN PILOTING

Even the most inexpensive plastic sextant can be a handy piloting tool in situations where the navigator needs to know his distance away from a charted object of known height, or from any of three charted objects that fall more or less in line.

The first case is called **distance off by vertical angle.** The navigator measures the angle subtended at his position by lines of sight taken to the top and bottom of an object. (When using a lighted aid, sights are taken to the light itself and to the object's base.) If the object's base is beyond the horizon, one must use Table XVI, with the visible horizon as base line. Table XVI, drawn from **Bowditch,** was constructed using a formula that allows both for refraction and for the curvature of the earth. If the object's base is visible, one may use either the table or the formula, $D = \dfrac{H \times 0.566}{A}$,

where **D** is the distance off in nautical miles, **H** is the height of the object in feet, and **A** is the observed sextant angle, corrected for index error, if any, and expressed in minutes and tenths of a minute of arc.

Example: A pilot sights an object whose charted height is 325 feet and whose base he can see. His sextant reading, corrected for index error, is 1°05.5'. With these data, the formula becomes

$$\frac{325 \times 0.566}{65.5} = 2.8 \text{ nautical miles.}$$

Another way of doing the same thing is by using the **horizon** or **depression angle,** defined as "the angle subtended between the horizon and the object's waterline." In this case, the formula is $D = \dfrac{EYE}{\tan H}$, where **D** is the distance off in feet, **EYE** is the observer's height of eye, and **H** is the sextant angle corrected for error and dip (for dip corrections, see page 52).

The second main use of the sextant is in determining **position by horizontal sextant angles.** Here one requires a shoreline with three identifiable, charted objects (height is of no consequence) that are more or less in line with one another (but not with the observer). The pilot determines (turning the sextant on its side) the angle between the lines of sight to the left and center objects and the corresponding angle using the right and center objects. These two angles are now set on a **three-arm protractor** (or **station pointer**), a device with one fixed, central arm and two that are movable. With the movable arms locked on either side of the central arm to express the required angles, the protractor is maneuvered on the chart until each of the three legs intersects the position of the appropriate charted object. The point at which the three legs join is the boat's position. If the boat is stationary, or moving quite slowly, this is a very accurate way of fixing her position.

One may also employ either vertical or horizontal sextant angles as danger angles when, for example, it is necessary to keep to seaward of a shallow, charted obstruction. If there is a charted object of known height ashore, measure on the chart the distance from the object to the seaward boundary of the hazardous area. Adding a bit for safety, use this distance (**D**) and the height of the object (**H**) in the formula, $\dfrac{H \times 0.566}{D}$, to extract the sextant angle in minutes and tenths. Thus, if the danger is one-half mile seaward of a charted object that is 150 feet high, then one should not allow the sextant to read more than about 2°30' (the closer inshore, the greater the angle). If the base of the object is over the horizon, use **D** and **H** to enter Table XVI, and read the appropriate vertical angle. If there are two charted objects ashore, one may use the horizontal angle between them as the danger angle. Again, the larger the angle, the closer to shore.

Dip Correction

This correction simply compensates for the fact that the eye of an observer in a boat is some distance above water when taking a sextant shot. The corrections below are always **subtracted** from the sextant reading. Heights are in feet, corrections in minutes and decimals.

Ht. of eye	Corrections	Ht. of eye	Corrections	Ht. of eye	Corrections
2	1.4	11	3.2	16	3.9
4	1.9	12	3.3	17	4.0
6	2.4	13	3.5	18	4.0
8	2.7	14	3.6	19	4.2
10	3.1	15	3.7	20	4.3

TABLE XVI. DISTANCE BY VERTICAL ANGLE (Bowditch, Table 9)

"Angle" refers to the sextant angle (corrected for index error and dip) subtended between the top of an object and the visible horizon. "Miles" are nautical miles.

Angle	Difference in feet between height of object and height of eye of observer										Angle
	25	30	35	40	45	50	60	70	80	90	
° ′	Miles	Miles	Miles	Miles	Miles	Miles	Miles	Miles	Miles	Miles	° ′
− 0 04	12.3	12.7	13.1	13.5	13.9	14.2	14.9	15.6	16.2	16.8	− 0 04
− 0 03	10.4	10.9	11.3	11.7	12.1	12.5	13.2	13.9	14.6	15.2	− 0 03
− 0 02	8.7	9.2	9.7	10.1	10.5	10.9	11.7	12.4	13.0	13.7	− 0 02
− 0 01	7.1	7.7	8.2	8.6	9.1	9.5	10.3	11.0	11.6	12.3	− 0 01
0 00	5.8	6.4	6.9	7.3	7.8	8.2	9.0	9.7	10.4	11.0	0 00
0 01	4.7	5.3	5.8	6.3	6.7	7.1	7.9	8.6	9.3	9.9	0 01
0 02	3.9	4.4	4.9	5.3	5.8	6.2	6.9	7.6	8.3	8.9	0 02
0 03	3.2	3.7	4.2	4.6	5.0	5.4	6.1	6.8	7.4	8.0	0 03
0 04	2.6	3.2	3.6	4.0	4.4	4.7	5.4	6.1	6.7	7.2	0 04
0 05	2.4	2.8	3.1	3.5	3.9	4.2	4.8	5.4	6.0	6.6	0 05
0 06	2.1	2.4	2.8	3.1	3.4	3.7	4.3	4.9	5.5	6.0	0 06
0 07	1.8	2.1	2.5	2.8	3.1	3.4	3.9	4.5	5.0	5.5	0 07
0 08	1.6	1.9	2.2	2.5	2.8	3.0	3.6	4.1	4.6	5.0	0 08
0 09	1.5	1.7	2.0	2.3	2.5	2.8	3.3	3.7	4.2	4.6	0 09
0 10	1.3	1.6	1.8	2.1	2.3	2.6	3.0	3.5	3.9	4.3	0 10
0 15	.9	1.1	1.3	1.5	1.6	1.8	2.1	2.5	2.8	3.1	0 15
0 20	.7	.8	1.0	1.1	1.2	1.4	1.6	1.9	2.2	2.4	0 20
0 25	.6	.7	.8	.9	1.0	1.1	1.3	1.5	1.8	2.0	0 25
0 30	.5	.6	.7	.7	.8	.9	1.1	1.3	1.5	1.7	0 30
0 35		.5	.6	.6	.7	.8	1.0	1.1	1.3	1.4	0 35
0 40			.5	.6	.6	.7	.8	1.0	1.1	1.3	0 40
0 45				.5	.6	.6	.7	.9	1.0	1.1	0 45
0 50				.5	.5	.6	.7	.8	.9	1.0	0 50
0 55					.5	.5	.6	.7	.8	.9	0 55
1 00						.5	.6	.7	.8	.8	1 00
1 10							.5	.6	.6	.7	1 10
1 20								.5	.6	.6	1 20
1 30									.5	.6	1 30
1 40									.5	.5	1 40
1 50										.5	1 50

Continued

DISTANCE BY VERTICAL ANGLE (Bowditch, Table 9)

| Angle | Difference in feet between height of object and height of eye of observer | | | | | | | | | | | Angle |
	100	120	140	160	180	200	250	300	350	400	450	
° ′	Miles	Miles	Miles	Miles	Miles	Miles	Miles	Miles	Miles	Miles	Miles	° ′
0 00	11.6	12.7	13.7	14.7	15.6	16.4	18.4	20.1	21.7	23.2	24.6	0 00
0 01	10.5	11.6	12.6	13.6	14.4	15.3	17.2	19.0	20.6	22.1	23.5	0 01
0 02	9.5	10.6	11.6	12.5	13.4	14.2	16.1	17.9	19.5	21.0	22.4	0 02
0 03	8.6	9.6	10.6	11.6	12.4	13.2	15.1	16.9	18.5	19.9	21.3	0 03
0 04	7.8	8.8	9.8	10.7	11.5	12.3	14.2	15.9	17.5	19.0	20.3	0 04
0 05	7.1	8.1	9.0	9.9	10.7	11.5	13.4	15.0	16.6	18.0	19.4	0 05
0 06	6.5	7.4	8.3	9.2	10.0	10.8	12.5	14.2	15.7	17.1	18.5	0 06
0 07	6.0	6.9	7.7	8.5	9.3	10.1	11.8	13.4	14.9	16.3	17.7	0 07
0 08	5.5	6.4	7.2	8.0	8.7	9.5	11.2	12.7	14.2	15.6	16.9	0 08
0 09	5.1	5.9	6.7	7.5	8.2	8.9	10.5	12.1	13.5	14.9	16.1	0 09
0 10	4.7	5.5	6.3	7.0	7.7	8.4	10.0	11.5	12.9	14.2	15.4	0 10
0 11	4.4	5.2	5.9	6.6	7.3	7.9	9.5	10.9	12.3	13.6	14.8	0 11
0 12	4.1	4.8	5.5	6.2	6.8	7.5	9.0	10.4	11.7	13.0	14.2	0 12
0 13	3.9	4.6	5.2	5.9	6.5	7.1	8.5	9.9	11.2	12.4	13.6	0 13
0 14	3.6	4.3	4.9	5.5	6.1	6.7	8.1	9.5	10.7	11.9	13.1	0 14
0 15	3.4	4.1	4.7	5.3	5.8	6.4	7.8	9.0	10.3	11.4	12.6	0 15
0 20	2.7	3.2	3.7	4.2	4.6	5.1	6.3	7.4	8.4	9.4	10.4	0 20
0 25	2.2	2.6	3.0	3.4	3.8	4.2	5.2	6.2	7.1	8.0	8.9	0 25
0 30	1.8	2.2	2.5	2.9	3.2	3.6	4.4	5.3	6.1	6.9	7.7	0 30
0 35	1.6	1.9	2.2	2.5	2.8	3.1	3.9	4.6	5.3	6.0	6.7	0 35
0 40	1.4	1.7	1.9	2.2	2.5	2.7	3.4	4.1	4.7	5.4	6.0	0 40
0 45	1.2	1.5	1.7	2.0	2.2	2.5	3.1	3.6	4.2	4.8	5.4	0 45
0 50	1.1	1.3	1.6	1.8	2.0	2.2	2.8	3.3	3.8	4.4	4.9	0 50
0 55	1.0	1.2	1.4	1.6	1.8	2.0	2.5	3.0	3.5	4.0	4.5	0 55
1 00	.9	1.1	1.3	1.5	1.7	1.9	2.3	2.8	3.2	3.7	4.1	1 00
1 10	.8	1.0	1.1	1.3	1.4	1.6	2.0	2.4	2.8	3.2	3.6	1 10
1 20	.7	.8	1.0	1.1	1.3	1.4	1.8	2.1	2.4	2.8	3.1	1 20
1 30	.6	.8	.9	1.0	1.1	1.2	1.6	1.9	2.2	2.5	2.8	1 30
1 40	.6	.7	.8	.9	1.0	1.1	1.4	1.7	2.0	2.2	2.5	1 40
1 50	.5	.6	.7	.8	.9	1.0	1.3	1.5	1.8	2.0	2.3	1 50
2 00	.5	.6	.7	.8	.8	.9	1.2	1.4	1.6	1.9	2.1	2 00
2 30		.5	.5	.6	.7	.8	.9	1.1	1.3	1.5	1.7	2 30
3 00				.5	.6	.6	.8	.9	1.1	1.3	1.4	3 00
3 30					.5	.5	.7	.8	.9	1.1	1.2	3 30
4 00						.5	.6	.7	.8	.9	1.1	4 00
4 30							.5	.6	.7	.8	.9	4 30
5 00							.5	.6	.7	.8	.8	5 00
6 00								.5	.5	.6	.7	6 00
7 00									.5	.5	.6	7 00
8 00										.5	.5	8 00
10 00												10 00

Continued

54

DISTANCE BY VERTICAL ANGLE (Bowditch, Table 9)

Angle	Difference in feet between height of object and height of eye of observer											Angle
	500	600	700	800	900	1000	1200	1400	1600	1800	2000	
° ′	Miles	Miles	Miles	Miles	Miles	Miles	Miles	Miles	Miles	Miles	Miles	° ′
0 05	20.7	23.1	25.4	27.4	29.4	31.3	34.7	37.9	40.9	43.7	46.3	0 05
0 06	19.8	22.2	24.4	26.5	28.4	30.3	33.7	36.9	39.8	42.6	45.3	0 06
0 07	18.9	21.3	23.5	25.5	27.5	29.3	32.7	35.9	38.9	41.6	44.3	0 07
0 08	18.1	20.5	22.6	24.7	26.6	28.4	31.8	35.0	37.9	40.7	43.3	0 08
0 09	17.4	19.7	21.8	23.8	25.7	27.5	30.9	34.0	37.0	39.7	42.3	0 09
0 10	16.7	18.9	21.0	23.0	24.9	26.7	30.0	33.1	36.0	38.8	41.4	0 10
0 11	16.0	18.2	20.3	22.3	24.1	25.9	29.2	32.3	35.2	37.9	40.5	0 11
0 12	15.3	17.5	19.6	21.5	23.4	25.1	28.4	31.5	34.3	37.0	39.6	0 12
0 13	14.8	16.9	18.9	20.8	22.6	24.4	27.6	30.7	33.5	36.2	38.7	0 13
0 14	14.2	16.3	18.3	20.2	22.0	23.7	26.9	29.9	32.7	35.3	37.9	0 14
0 15	13.7	15.7	17.7	19.5	21.3	23.0	26.2	29.1	31.9	34.6	37.1	0 15
0 17	12.7	14.7	16.5	18.3	20.0	21.7	24.8	27.7	30.4	33.0	35.4	0 17
0 20	11.4	13.3	15.0	16.7	18.4	19.9	22.9	25.7	28.4	30.9	33.3	0 20
0 25	9.7	11.4	13.0	14.6	16.1	17.5	20.3	22.9	25.4	27.8	30.1	0 25
0 30	8.4	9.9	11.4	12.8	14.2	15.5	18.1	20.5	22.9	25.1	27.3	0 30
0 35	7.4	8.8	10.1	11.4	12.6	13.9	16.2	18.5	20.7	22.8	24.9	0 35
0 40	6.6	7.8	9.0	10.2	11.4	12.5	14.7	16.8	18.9	20.9	22.8	0 40
0 45	6.0	7.1	8.2	9.3	10.3	11.4	13.4	15.4	17.3	19.2	21.0	0 45
0 50	5.4	6.4	7.5	8.4	9.4	10.4	12.3	14.2	16.0	17.7	19.5	0 50
0 55	5.0	5.9	6.8	7.8	8.7	9.6	11.4	13.1	14.8	16.5	18.1	0 55
1 00	4.6	5.5	6.3	7.2	8.0	8.9	10.5	12.2	13.8	15.3	16.9	1 00
1 10	3.9	4.7	5.5	6.2	7.0	7.7	9.2	10.6	12.1	13.5	14.8	1 10
1 20	3.5	4.2	4.8	5.5	6.2	6.8	8.1	9.4	10.7	12.0	13.2	1 20
1 30	3.1	3.7	4.3	4.9	5.5	6.1	7.3	8.5	9.6	10.8	11.9	1 30
1 40	2.8	3.3	3.9	4.4	5.0	5.5	6.6	7.7	8.7	9.8	10.8	1 40
1 50	2.5	3.0	3.6	4.1	4.5	5.0	6.0	7.0	8.0	9.0	9.9	1 50
2 00	2.3	2.8	3.3	3.7	4.2	4.6	5.5	6.5	7.4	8.2	9.1	2 00
2 30	1.9	2.2	2.6	3.0	3.4	3.7	4.5	5.2	5.9	6.7	7.4	2 30
3 00	1.6	1.9	2.2	2.5	2.8	3.1	3.7	4.4	5.0	5.6	6.2	3 00
3 30	1.3	1.6	1.9	2.1	2.4	2.7	3.2	3.7	4.3	4.8	5.3	3 30
4 00	1.2	1.4	1.6	1.9	2.1	2.3	2.8	3.3	3.7	4.2	4.7	4 00
5 00	.9	1.1	1.3	1.5	1.7	1.9	2.3	2.6	3.0	3.4	3.7	5 00
6 00	.8	.9	1.1	1.3	1.4	1.6	1.9	2.2	2.5	2.8	3.1	6 00
7 00	.7	.8	.9	1.1	1.2	1.3	1.6	1.9	2.1	2.4	2.7	7 00
8 00	.6	.7	.8	.9	1.1	1.2	1.4	1.6	1.9	2.1	2.3	8 00
10 00	.5	.6	.7	.7	.8	.9	1.1	1.3	1.5	1.7	1.9	10 00
12 00		.5	.5	.6	.7	.8	.9	1.1	1.2	1.4	1.5	12 00
15 00				.5	.6	.6	.7	.9	1.0	1.1	1.2	15 00
20 00						.5	.5	.6	.7	.8	.9	20 00
25 00								.5	.6	.6	.7	25 00
30 00									.5	.5	.6	30 00

VISIBILITY OF DISTANT OBJECTS

There are four conditions governing how far an object, lighted or unlighted, may be seen: its own height, the height of the observer, its intrinsic visibility (in terms of brightness, color, and contrast), and the atmospheric conditions at the time of the observation. Leaving aside the last area, which is relatively unpredictable, we can come to grips with the other three.

The effects of height — either the observer's or the object's — on visibility really result, of course, from the curvature of the earth. When speaking of an aid to navigation, we customarily refer to the maximum possible distance of visibility, given the observer's height above water level, as the **geographic range.** To judge the geographic range of any object (assuming optimum viewing conditions), one must take the distance from the top of the object to the horizon from Table XVII, and add to it the distance of the horizon from the observer, which can also be taken from Table XVII. Do not, however, make the mistake of adding the height of the object to the height of the observer's eye and then consulting the table.

TABLE XVII. DISTANCE OF THE HORIZON FROM VARIOUS HEIGHTS

Height (Feet)	Nautical Miles	Statute Miles	Height (Feet)	Nautical Miles	Statute Miles
1	1.1	1.3	30	6.3	7.2
2	1.6	1.9	35	6.8	7.8
3	2.0	2.3	40	7.2	8.3
4	2.3	2.6	45	7.7	8.8
5	2.6	2.9	50	8.1	9.3
6	2.8	3.2	55	8.5	9.8
7	3.0	3.5	60	8.9	10.2
8	3.2	3.7	65	9.2	10.6
9	3.4	4.0	70	9.6	11.0
10	3.6	4.2	75	9.9	11.4
11	3.8	4.4	80	10.2	11.8
12	4.0	4.6	90	10.9	12.5
13	4.1	4.7	100	11.4	13.2
14	4.3	4.9	125	12.8	14.7
15	4.4	5.1	150	14.0	16.1
16	4.6	5.3	200	16.2	18.6
17	4.7	5.4	250	18.1	20.8
18	4.9	5.6	300	19.8	22.8
19	5.0	5.7	350	21.4	24.6
20	5.1	5.9	400	22.9	26.3
21	5.2	6.0	500	25.6	29.4
22	5.4	6.2	600	28.0	32.3
23	5.5	6.3	700	30.3	34.8
24	5.6	6.5	800	32.4	37.3
25	5.7	6.6	900	34.3	39.9

Example: You are standing on the deck of a small vessel and estimate your eye height at 10 feet. How far off might you expect to see a light 27 feet high? Your own 10 feet of height give you a horizon 3.6 nautical miles distant. Add to that 5.9 miles for the object itself, and you should expect to see it at about 9.5 miles — not 7 miles, which is the result you would get from adding 10 and 27 and entering Table XVII with their sum. The sketch below should make the reason for this clear.

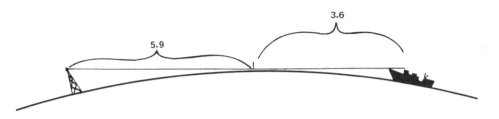

In the **Light List,** published by the U.S. Coast Guard, is noted the **nominal range** of each major aid to navigation — the distance at which it can be seen in clear weather, taking only the light's candlepower and color into consideration. All other things being equal, white lights are visible farthest, followed by red, and finally, green. Where a major light has a pattern using more than one color, the nominal range of each color is given. Such a light obviously will present a confusing pattern to a viewer near the maximum range of visibility.

Heights of lighted aids are, of course, given on the chart and in the **Light List** with reference to the height of the light itself at high water; at other stages of the tide they may appear to be considerably taller. The supporting structure of a lighted aid may be higher than the light, but seldom by a consequential amount.

DISTANCE OF AN OBJECT BY TWO BEARINGS

To use Table XVIII, you need a compass and a reliable speedometer or log. Using these instruments, take two distinct bearings on a fixed object as you pass by it, noting the distance run between the two bearings.

In Table XVIII, the columns refer to the **difference** between the vessel's course and the first bearing; the horizontal lines refer to the **difference** between the vessel's course and the second bearing. Enter the table with the two differences, and at the intersection of the designated line and column you will find two numbers. To find the distance off at the time of the second bearing, multiply the distance run between bearings by the left-hand number. To find the distance off at the time the vessel is abeam, multiply the distance run by the right-hand number.

Example: Your vessel is proceeding on a course of 100° at 6 knots. At 1312 you take a bearing on a lighthouse off the starboard bow. Your bearing is 150° psc (per standard compass). At 1324 you take another bearing on the lighthouse, and it is 170° psc. In 12 minutes your vessel will have traveled 1.2 nautical miles.

The difference between the course and the first bearing is 50°, and the difference between the course and the second bearing is 70°. Entering the table with these figures, you find that the two numbers at the point of intersection are 2.2 and 2.1. The first figure, 2.2, multiplied by the distance traveled, 1.2, results in a distance off at the time of the second bearing (1324) of 2.7 nautical miles. Using 2.1 results in a distance off of 2.5 miles at the time your vessel comes abeam of the lighthouse.

Example: You are on a course of 275° and your speed is 15 knots. At 0910 your bearing on a distant stack is 312°. At 0915 the bearing is 350°.

The difference between your course and the first bearing is 37°. The distance traveled between bearings is 1.25 nautical miles. The difference between your course and the second bearing is 75°. The stack is 1.2 nautical miles away, both at the time of the second bearing and when it is abeam.

Note 1: If the distance between bearings is exactly one mile, then the factors in Table XVIII require no working and are themselves the required answers.

Note 2: Certain frequently used combinations of first and second bearings lend themselves to convenient shortcut solutions. These are presented in the following section.

TABLE XVIII. DISTANCE OF AN OBJECT DETERMINED BY TWO BEARINGS

Difference between course and 2nd bearing (left column) vs. Difference between course and first bearing (top).

Diff (2nd)	20°		22°		24°		26°		28°		30°		32°	
30°	2.0	1.0												
32	1.6	0.9	2.2	1.1										
34	1.4	0.8	1.8	1.0	2.3	1.3								
36	1.2	0.7	1.6	0.9	2.0	1.2	2.5	1.5						
38	1.1	0.7	1.4	0.8	1.7	1.0	2.1	1.3	2.7	1.7				
40	1.0	0.6	1.2	0.8	1.5	1.0	1.8	1.2	2.3	1.4	2.9	1.8		
42	0.9	0.6	1.1	0.7	1.3	0.9	1.6	1.1	1.9	1.3	2.4	1.6	3.1	2.0
44	0.8	0.6	1.0	0.7	1.2	0.8	1.4	1.0	1.7	1.2	2.1	1.4	2.6	1.8
46	0.8	0.6	0.9	0.7	1.1	0.8	1.3	0.9	1.5	1.1	1.8	1.3	2.2	1.6
48	0.7	0.5	0.8	0.6	1.0	0.7	1.2	0.9	1.4	1.0	1.6	1.2	1.9	1.4
50	0.7	0.5	0.8	0.6	0.9	0.7	1.1	0.8	1.2	1.0	1.5	1.1	1.7	1.3
52	0.6	0.5	0.8	0.6	0.9	0.7	1.0	0.8	1.2	0.9	1.3	1.0	1.6	1.2
54	0.6	0.5	0.7	0.6	0.8	0.7	0.9	0.8	1.1	0.9	1.2	1.0	1.4	1.1
56	0.6	0.5	0.7	0.6	0.8	0.6	0.9	0.7	1.0	0.8	1.1	1.0	1.3	1.1
58	0.6	0.5	0.6	0.5	0.7	0.6	0.8	0.7	0.9	0.8	1.1	0.9	1.2	1.0
60	0.5	0.5	0.6	0.5	0.7	0.6	0.8	0.7	0.9	0.8	1.0	0.9	1.1	1.0
62	0.5	0.5	0.6	0.5	0.7	0.6	0.8	0.7	0.8	0.7	0.9	0.8	1.1	0.9
64	0.5	0.4	0.6	0.5	0.6	0.6	0.7	0.6	0.8	0.7	0.9	0.8	1.0	0.9
66	0.5	0.4	0.5	0.5	0.6	0.6	0.7	0.6	0.8	0.7	0.8	0.8	1.0	0.9
68	0.5	0.4	0.5	0.5	0.6	0.5	0.7	0.6	0.7	0.7	0.8	0.8	0.9	0.8
70	0.4	0.4	0.5	0.5	0.6	0.5	0.6	0.6	0.7	0.7	0.8	0.7	0.9	0.8
72	0.4	0.4	0.5	0.5	0.6	0.5	0.6	0.6	0.7	0.6	0.8	0.7	0.8	0.8
74	0.4	0.4	0.5	0.5	0.5	0.5	0.6	0.6	0.6	0.6	0.7	0.7	0.8	0.8
76	0.4	0.4	0.5	0.4	0.5	0.5	0.6	0.6	0.6	0.6	0.7	0.7	0.8	0.7
78	0.4	0.4	0.4	0.4	0.5	0.5	0.6	0.5	0.6	0.6	0.7	0.7	0.7	0.7
80	0.4	0.4	0.4	0.4	0.5	0.5	0.5	0.5	0.6	0.6	0.6	0.6	0.7	0.7
82	0.4	0.4	0.4	0.4	0.5	0.5	0.5	0.5	0.6	0.6	0.6	0.6	0.7	0.7
84	0.4	0.4	0.4	0.4	0.5	0.5	0.5	0.5	0.6	0.6	0.6	0.6	0.7	0.7
86	0.4	0.4	0.4	0.4	0.5	0.5	0.5	0.5	0.6	0.6	0.6	0.6	0.7	0.6
88	0.4	0.4	0.4	0.4	0.4	0.4	0.5	0.5	0.5	0.5	0.6	0.6	0.6	0.6
90	0.4	0.4	0.4	0.4	0.4	0.4	0.5	0.5	0.5	0.5	0.6	0.6	0.6	0.6
92	0.4	0.4	0.4	0.4	0.4	0.4	0.5	0.5	0.5	0.5	0.6	0.6	0.6	0.6
94	0.4	0.4	0.4	0.4	0.4	0.4	0.5	0.5	0.5	0.5	0.6	0.6	0.6	0.6
96	0.4	0.4	0.4	0.4	0.4	0.4	0.5	0.5	0.5	0.5	0.5	0.5	0.6	0.6
98	0.4	0.4	0.4	0.4	0.4	0.4	0.5	0.5	0.5	0.5	0.5	0.5	0.6	0.6
100	0.4	0.3	0.4	0.4	0.4	0.4	0.5	0.4	0.5	0.5	0.5	0.5	0.6	0.6
102	0.4	0.3	0.4	0.4	0.4	0.4	0.4	0.4	0.5	0.5	0.5	0.5	0.6	0.6
104	0.3	0.3	0.4	0.4	0.4	0.4	0.4	0.4	0.5	0.5	0.5	0.5	0.6	0.5
106	0.3	0.3	0.4	0.4	0.4	0.4	0.4	0.4	0.5	0.5	0.5	0.5	0.6	0.5
108	0.3	0.3	0.4	0.4	0.4	0.4	0.4	0.4	0.5	0.4	0.5	0.5	0.6	0.5
110	0.3	0.3	0.4	0.4	0.4	0.4	0.4	0.4	0.5	0.4	0.5	0.5	0.5	0.5
112	0.3	0.3	0.4	0.4	0.4	0.4	0.4	0.4	0.5	0.4	0.5	0.5	0.5	0.5
114	0.3	0.3	0.4	0.3	0.4	0.4	0.4	0.4	0.5	0.4	0.5	0.5	0.5	0.5
116	0.3	0.3	0.4	0.3	0.4	0.4	0.4	0.4	0.5	0.4	0.5	0.4	0.5	0.5
118	0.4	0.3	0.4	0.3	0.4	0.4	0.4	0.4	0.5	0.4	0.5	0.4	0.5	0.5
120	0.4	0.3	0.4	0.3	0.4	0.4	0.4	0.4	0.5	0.4	0.5	0.4	0.5	0.5
122	0.4	0.3	0.4	0.3	0.4	0.4	0.4	0.4	0.5	0.4	0.5	0.4	0.5	0.4
124	0.4	0.3	0.4	0.3	0.4	0.3	0.4	0.4	0.5	0.4	0.5	0.4	0.5	0.4
126	0.4	0.3	0.4	0.3	0.4	0.3	0.4	0.4	0.5	0.4	0.5	0.4	0.5	0.4
128	0.4	0.3	0.4	0.3	0.4	0.3	0.4	0.3	0.5	0.4	0.5	0.4	0.5	0.4

Continued

DISTANCE OF AN OBJECT DETERMINED BY TWO BEARINGS

Difference between course and first bearing

Difference between course and 2nd bearing

	34°		36°		38°		40°		42°		44°		46°	
44°	3.2	2.2												
46	2.7	1.9	3.4	2.4										
48	2.3	1.7	1.8	2.1	3.6	2.6								
50	2.0	1.6	2.4	1.9	3.0	2.3	3.7	2.8						
52	1.8	1.4	2.1	1.7	2.5	2.0	3.1	2.4	3.8	3.0				
54	1.6	1.3	1.9	1.5	2.2	1.8	2.7	2.2	3.2	2.6	4.0	3.2		
56	1.5	1.2	1.7	1.4	2.0	1.6	2.3	1.9	2.8	2.3	3.3	2.8	4.1	3.4
58	1.4	1.2	1.6	1.3	1.8	1.5	2.1	1.8	2.4	2.1	2.9	2.4	3.5	2.9
60	1.3	1.1	1.4	1.2	1.6	1.4	1.9	1.6	2.2	1.9	2.5	2.2	3.0	2.6
62	1.2	1.0	1.3	1.2	1.5	1.3	1.7	1.5	2.0	1.7	2.2	2.0	2.6	2.3
64	1.1	1.0	1.2	1.1	1.4	1.3	1.6	1.4	1.8	1.6	2.0	1.8	2.3	2.1
66	1.1	1.0	1.2	1.1	1.3	1.2	1.5	1.3	1.5	1.5	1.8	1.7	2.1	1.9
68	1.0	0.9	1.1	1.0	1.2	1.1	1.4	1.3	1.5	1.4	1.7	1.6	1.9	1.8
70	1.0	0.9	1.0	1.0	1.2	1.1	1.3	1.2	1.4	1.3	1.6	1.5	1.8	1.7
72	0.9	0.9	1.0	1.0	1.1	1.0	1.2	1.2	1.3	1.3	1.5	1.4	1.6	1.6
74	0.9	0.8	1.0	0.9	1.0	1.0	1.2	1.1	1.3	1.2	1.4	1.3	1.5	1.5
76	0.8	0.8	0.9	0.9	1.0	1.0	1.1	1.1	1.2	1.2	1.3	1.3	1.4	1.4
78	0.8	0.8	0.9	0.9	1.0	0.9	1.0	1.0	1.1	1.1	1.2	1.2	1.4	1.3
80	0.8	0.8	0.8	0.8	0.9	0.9	1.0	1.0	1.1	1.1	1.2	1.2	1.3	1.3
82	0.8	0.8	0.8	0.8	0.9	0.9	1.0	1.0	1.0	1.0	1.1	1.1	1.2	1.2
84	0.7	0.7	0.8	0.8	0.9	0.8	0.9	0.9	1.0	1.0	1.1	1.1	1.2	1.2
86	0.7	0.7	0.8	0.8	0.8	0.8	0.9	0.9	1.0	1.0	1.0	1.0	1.1	1.1
88	0.7	0.7	0.8	0.8	0.8	0.8	0.9	0.9	0.9	0.9	1.0	1.0	1.1	1.1
90	0.7	0.7	0.7	0.7	0.8	0.8	0.8	0.8	0.9	0.9	1.0	1.0	1.0	1.0
92	0.7	0.7	0.7	0.7	0.8	0.8	0.8	0.8	0.9	0.9	0.9	0.9	1.0	1.0
94	0.5	0.6	0.7	0.7	0.7	0.7	0.8	0.8	0.8	0.8	0.9	0.9	1.0	1.0
96	0.6	0.6	0.7	0.7	0.7	0.7	0.8	0.8	0.8	0.8	0.9	0.9	0.9	0.9
98	0.6	0.6	0.7	0.7	0.7	0.7	0.8	0.8	0.8	0.8	0.9	0.8	0.9	0.9
100	0.6	0.6	0.6	0.6	0.7	0.7	0.7	0.7	0.8	0.8	0.8	0.8	0.9	0.9
102	0.6	0.6	0.6	0.6	0.7	0.7	0.7	0.7	0.8	0.8	0.8	0.8	0.9	0.8
104	0.6	0.6	0.6	0.6	0.7	0.6	0.7	0.7	0.8	0.7	0.8	0.8	0.8	0.8
106	0.6	0.6	0.6	0.6	0.7	0.6	0.7	0.7	0.7	0.7	0.8	0.8	0.8	0.8
108	0.6	0.6	0.6	0.6	0.7	0.6	0.7	0.7	0.7	0.7	0.8	0.7	0.8	0.8
110	0.6	0.5	0.6	0.6	0.6	0.6	0.7	0.6	0.7	0.7	0.8	0.7	0.8	0.8
112	0.6	0.5	0.6	0.6	0.6	0.6	0.7	0.6	0.7	0.7	0.8	0.7	0.8	0.7
114	0.6	0.5	0.6	0.6	0.6	0.6	0.6	0.6	0.7	0.6	0.7	0.7	0.8	0.7
116	0.6	0.5	0.6	0.5	0.6	0.6	0.7	0.6	0.7	0.6	0.7	0.7	0.8	0.7
118	0.6	0.5	0.6	0.5	0.6	0.6	0.7	0.6	0.7	0.7	0.7	0.6	0.8	0.7
120	0.6	0.5	0.6	0.5	0.6	0.5	0.6	0.6	0.7	0.6	0.7	0.6	0.8	0.6
122	0.6	0.5	0.6	0.5	0.6	0.5	0.6	0.6	0.7	0.6	0.7	0.6	0.7	0.6
124	0.6	0.5	0.6	0.5	0.6	0.5	0.6	0.5	0.7	0.6	0.7	0.6	0.7	0.6
126	0.6	0.4	0.6	0.5	0.6	0.5	0.6	0.5	0.7	0.5	0.7	0.6	0.7	0.6
128	0.6	0.4	0.6	0.5	0.6	0.5	0.6	0.5	0.7	0.5	0.7	0.6	0.7	0.6
130	0.6	0.4	0.6	0.4	0.6	0.5	0.6	0.5	0.7	0.5	0.7	0.5	0.7	0.6
132	0.6	0.4	0.6	0.4	0.6	0.5	0.6	0.5	0.7	0.5	0.7	0.5	0.7	0.5
134	0.6	0.4	0.6	0.4	0.6	0.4	0.6	0.5	0.7	0.5	0.7	0.5	0.7	0.5
136	0.6	0.4	0.6	0.4	0.6	0.4	0.6	0.4	0.7	0.5	0.7	0.5	0.7	0.5
138	0.6	0.4	0.6	0.4	0.6	0.4	0.6	0.4	0.7	0.4	0.7	0.5	0.7	0.5

Continued

60

DISTANCE OF AN OBJECT DETERMINED BY TWO BEARINGS

Difference between course and 2nd bearing →

	48°		50°		52°		54°		56°		58°		60°	
58°	4.3	3.6												
60	3.6	3.1	4.4	3.8										
62	3.1	2.7	3.7	3.2	4.5	4.0								
64	2.7	2.4	3.2	2.8	2.8	3.4	4.7	4.2						
66	2.4	2.2	2.8	2.5	3.3	3.0	4.0	3.6	4.8	4.4				
68	2.2	2.0	2.5	2.3	2.9	2.6	3.3	3.1	4.0	3.7	4.9	4.5		
70	2.0	1.9	2.2	2.1	2.6	2.4	2.9	2.8	3.4	3.2	4.1	3.8	5.0	4.7
72	1.8	1.7	2.0	1.9	2.3	2.2	2.6	2.5	3.0	2.9	3.5	3.3	4.2	4.0
74	1.7	1.6	1.9	1.8	2.1	2.0	2.4	2.3	2.7	2.6	3.1	3.0	3.6	3.4
76	1.6	1.5	1.8	1.7	1.9	1.9	2.2	2.1	2.4	2.4	2.7	2.7	3.1	3.0
78	1.5	1.4	1.6	1.6	1.8	1.8	2.0	2.0	2.2	2.2	2.5	2.4	2.8	2.7
80	1.4	1.4	1.5	1.5	1.7	1.6	1.8	1.8	2.0	2.0	2.3	2.2	2.5	2.5
82	1.3	1.3	1.4	1.4	1.6	1.6	1.7	1.7	1.9	1.9	2.1	2.1	2.3	2.3
84	1.3	1.3	1.4	1.4	1.5	1.5	1.6	1.6	1.8	1.8	1.9	1.9	2.1	2.1
86	1.2	1.2	1.3	1.3	1.4	1.4	1.5	1.5	1.7	1.6	1.8	1.8	2.0	2.0
88	1.2	1.2	1.2	1.2	1.3	1.3	1.4	1.4	1.6	1.6	1.7	1.7	1.8	1.8
90	1.1	1.1	1.2	1.2	1.3	1.3	1.4	1.4	1.5	1.5	1.6	1.6	1.7	1.7
92	1.1	1.1	1.1	1.1	1.2	1.2	1.3	1.3	1.4	1.4	1.5	1.5	1.6	1.6
94	1.0	1.0	1.1	1.1	1.2	1.2	1.3	1.3	1.4	1.3	1.4	1.4	1.5	1.5
96	1.0	1.0	1.1	1.1	1.1	1.1	1.2	1.2	1.3	1.3	1.4	1.4	1.5	1.5
98	1.0	1.0	1.0	1.0	1.1	1.1	1.2	1.2	1.2	1.2	1.3	1.3	1.4	1.4
100	0.9	0.9	1.0	1.0	1.1	1.0	1.1	1.1	1.2	1.2	1.3	1.2	1.4	1.3
102	0.9	0.9	1.0	1.0	1.0	1.0	1.1	1.1	1.2	1.1	1.2	1.2	1.3	1.3
104	0.9	0.9	1.0	0.9	1.0	1.0	1.1	1.0	1.1	1.1	1.2	1.1	1.2	1.2
106	0.9	0.8	0.9	0.9	1.0	0.9	1.0	1.0	1.1	1.0	1.1	1.1	1.2	1.2
108	0.9	0.8	0.9	0.9	1.0	0.9	1.0	1.0	1.0	1.0	1.1	1.0	1.2	1.1
110	0.8	0.8	0.9	0.8	0.9	0.9	1.0	0.9	1.0	1.0	1.1	1.0	1.1	1.1
112	0.8	0.8	0.9	0.8	0.9	0.8	1.0	0.9	1.0	0.9	1.0	1.0	1.1	1.0
114	0.8	0.7	0.8	0.8	0.9	0.8	0.9	0.8	1.0	0.9	1.0	0.9	1.1	1.0
116	0.8	0.7	0.8	0.8	0.9	0.8	0.9	0.8	1.0	0.8	1.0	0.9	1.0	0.9
118	0.8	0.7	0.8	0.7	0.9	0.8	0.9	0.8	0.9	0.8	1.0	0.9	1.0	0.9
120	0.8	0.7	0.8	0.7	0.8	0.7	0.9	0.8	0.9	0.8	1.0	0.8	1.0	0.9
122	0.8	0.7	0.8	0.7	0.8	0.7	0.9	0.7	0.9	0.8	1.0	0.8	1.0	0.8
124	0.8	0.6	0.8	0.7	0.8	0.7	0.9	0.7	0.9	0.7	0.9	0.8	1.0	0.8
126	0.8	0.6	0.8	0.6	0.8	0.7	0.8	0.7	0.9	0.7	0.9	0.7	1.0	0.8
128	0.8	0.6	0.8	0.6	0.8	0.6	0.8	0.7	0.9	0.7	0.9	0.7	0.9	0.7
130	0.8	0.6	0.8	0.6	0.8	0.6	0.8	0.6	0.9	0.7	0.9	0.7	0.9	0.7
132	0.8	0.6	0.8	0.6	0.8	0.6	0.8	0.6	0.8	0.6	0.9	0.7	0.9	0.7
134	0.7	0.5	0.8	0.6	0.8	0.6	0.8	0.6	0.8	0.6	0.9	0.6	0.9	0.6
136	0.7	0.5	0.8	0.5	0.8	0.6	0.8	0.6	0.8	0.6	0.9	0.6	0.9	0.6
138	0.7	0.5	0.8	0.5	0.8	0.5	0.8	0.5	0.8	0.6	0.9	0.6	0.9	0.6
140	0.7	0.5	0.8	0.5	0.8	0.5	0.8	0.5	0.8	0.5	0.9	0.6	0.9	0.6
142	0.7	0.5	0.8	0.5	0.8	0.5	0.8	0.5	0.8	0.5	0.8	0.5	0.9	0.6
144	0.8	0.5	0.8	0.4	0.8	0.5	0.8	0.5	0.8	0.5	0.8	0.5	0.9	0.5
146	0.8	0.4	0.8	0.4	0.8	0.4	0.8	0.4	0.8	0.5	0.8	0.5	0.9	0.5
148	0.8	0.4	0.8	0.4	0.8	0.4	0.8	0.4	0.8	0.4	0.8	0.4	0.9	0.5
150	0.8	0.4	0.8	0.4	0.8	0.4	0.8	0.4	0.8	0.4	0.8	0.4	0.9	0.4
152	0.8	0.4	0.8	0.4	0.8	0.4	0.8	0.4	0.8	0.4	0.8	0.4	0.9	0.4
154	0.8	0.3	0.8	0.4	0.8	0.4	0.8	0.4	0.8	0.4	0.8	0.4	0.9	0.4
156	0.8	0.3	0.8	0.3	0.8	0.3	0.8	0.3	0.8	0.3	0.8	0.4	0.9	0.4
158	0.8	0.3	0.8	0.3	0.8	0.3	0.8	0.3	0.8	0.3	0.8	0.3	0.9	0.3
160	0.8	0.3	0.8	0.3	0.8	0.3	0.8	0.3	0.8	0.3	0.8	0.3	0.9	0.3

Difference between course and first bearing

Continued

DISTANCE OF AN OBJECT DETERMINED BY TWO BEARINGS

Difference between course and 2nd bearing

	62°		64°		66°		68°		70°		72°	
72°	5.1	4.8										
74	4.2	4.1	5.2	5.0								
76	3.6	3.5	4.3	4.2	5.3	5.1						
78	3.2	3.1	3.7	3.6	4.4	4.3	5.3	5.2				
80	2.9	2.8	3.3	3.2	3.8	3.7	4.5	4.4	5.4	5.3		
82	2.6	2.6	2.9	2.8	3.3	3.3	3.8	3.8	4.5	4.5	5.5	5.4
84	2.4	2.3	2.6	2.6	3.0	2.9	3.4	3.4	3.9	3.9	4.6	4.6
86	2.2	2.2	2.4	2.4	2.7	3.7	3.0	3.0	3.4	3.4	3.9	3.9
88	2.0	2.0	2.2	2.2	2.4	2.4	2.7	2.7	3.0	3.0	3.4	3.4
90	1.9	1.9	2.0	2.0	2.2	2.2	2.5	2.5	2.8	2.8	3.1	3.1
92	1.8	1.8	1.9	1.9	2.1	2.1	2.3	2.3	2.5	2.5	2.8	2.8
94	1.7	1.7	1.8	1.8	2.0	1.9	2.1	2.1	2.3	2.3	2.5	2.5
96	1.6	1.6	1.7	1.7	1.8	1.8	2.0	2.0	2.1	2.1	2.3	2.3
98	1.5	1.5	1.6	1.6	1.7	1.7	1.8	1.8	2.0	2.0	2.2	2.2
100	1.4	1.4	1.5	1.5	1.6	1.6	1.8	1.7	1.9	1.8	2.0	2.0
102	1.4	1.3	1.5	1.4	1.6	1.5	1.7	1.6	1.8	1.7	1.9	1.9
104	1.3	1.3	1.4	1.4	1.5	1.4	1.6	1.5	1.7	1.6	1.8	1.7
106	1.3	1.2	1.3	1.3	1.4	1.4	1.5	1.4	1.6	1.5	1.7	1.6
108	1.2	1.2	1.3	1.2	1.4	1.3	1.4	1.4	1.5	1.4	1.6	1.5
110	1.2	1.1	1.2	1.2	1.3	1.2	1.4	1.3	1.5	1.4	1.5	1.4
112	1.2	1.1	1.2	1.1	1.3	1.2	1.3	1.2	1.4	1.3	1.5	1.4
114	1.1	1.0	1.2	1.1	1.2	1.1	1.3	1.2	1.4	1.2	1.4	1.3
116	1.1	1.0	1.1	1.0	1.2	1.1	1.2	1.1	1.3	1.2	1.4	1.2
118	1.1	0.9	1.1	1.0	1.2	1.0	1.2	1.1	1.3	1.1	1.3	1.2
120	1.0	0.9	1.1	0.9	1.1	1.0	1.2	1.0	1.2	1.1	1.3	1.1
122	1.0	0.9	1.1	0.9	1.1	0.9	1.2	1.0	1.2	1.0	1.2	1.0
124	1.0	0.8	1.0	0.9	1.1	0.9	1.1	0.9	1.2	1.0	1.2	1.0
126	1.0	0.8	1.0	0.8	1.0	0.8	1.1	0.9	1.1	0.9	1.2	1.0
128	1.0	0.8	1.0	0.8	1.0	0.8	1.1	0.8	1.1	0.9	1.2	0.9
130	1.0	0.7	1.0	0.8	1.0	0.8	1.0	0.8	1.1	0.8	1.1	0.9
132	0.9	0.7	1.0	0.7	1.0	0.7	1.0	0.8	1.1	0.8	1.1	0.8
134	0.9	0.7	1.0	0.7	1.0	0.7	1.0	0.7	1.0	0.8	1.1	0.8
136	0.9	0.6	1.0	0.7	1.0	0.7	1.0	0.7	1.0	0.7	1.1	0.7
138	0.9	0.6	0.9	0.6	1.0	0.6	1.0	0.7	1.0	0.7	1.0	0.7
140	0.9	0.6	0.9	0.6	1.0	0.6	1.0	0.6	1.0	0.6	1.0	0.7
142	0.9	0.6	0.9	0.6	0.9	0.6	1.0	0.6	1.0	0.6	1.0	0.6
144	0.9	0.5	0.9	0.5	0.9	0.6	0.9	0.6	1.0	0.6	1.0	0.6
146	0.9	0.5	0.9	0.5	0.9	0.5	0.9	0.5	1.0	0.5	1.0	0.6
148	0.9	0.5	0.9	0.5	0.9	0.5	0.9	0.5	1.0	0.5	1.0	0.5
150	0.9	0.4	0.9	0.4	0.9	0.5	0.9	0.5	1.0	0.5	1.0	0.5
152	0.9	0.4	0.9	0.4	0.9	0.4	0.9	0.4	1.0	0.4	1.0	0.4
154	0.9	0.4	0.9	0.4	0.9	0.4	0.9	0.4	0.9	0.4	1.0	0.4
156	0.9	0.4	0.9	0.4	0.9	0.4	0.9	0.4	0.9	0.4	1.0	0.4
158	0.9	0.3	0.9	0.3	0.9	0.3	0.9	0.4	0.9	0.4	1.0	0.4
160	0.9	0.3	0.9	0.3	0.9	0.3	0.9	0.3	0.9	0.3	1.0	0.3

Continued

DISTANCE OF AN OBJECT DETERMINED BY TWO BEARINGS

	74°		76°		78°		80°		82°		84°		86°	
	Difference between course and first bearing													
84°	5.5	5.5												
86	4.6	4.6	5.6	5.6										
88	4.0	4.0	4.7	4.7	5.6	5.6								
90	3.5	3.5	4.0	4.0	4.7	4.7	5.7	5.7						
92	3.1	3.1	3.5	3.5	4.0	4.0	4.7	4.7	5.7	5.7				
94	2.8	2.8	3.1	3.1	3.6	3.5	4.1	4.1	4.8	4.8	5.7	5.7		
96	2.6	2.6	2.8	2.8	3.2	3.2	3.6	3.6	4.1	4.1	4.8	4.8	5.7	5.7
98	2.4	2.3	2.6	2.6	2.9	2.8	3.2	3.2	3.6	3.6	4.1	4.1	4.8	4.8
100	2.2	2.2	2.4	2.4	2.6	2.6	2.9	2.8	3.2	3.2	3.6	3.6	4.1	4.1
102	2.0	2.0	2.2	2.2	2.4	2.4	2.6	2.6	2.9	2.8	3.2	3.2	3.6	3.5
104	1.9	1.9	2.1	2.0	2.2	2.2	2.4	2.4	2.6	2.6	2.9	2.8	3.2	3.1
106	1.8	1.7	1.9	1.9	2.1	2.0	2.2	2.2	2.4	2.3	2.6	2.6	2.9	2.8
108	1.7	1.6	1.8	1.7	2.0	1.9	2.1	2.0	2.3	2.2	2.4	2.3	2.7	2.5
110	1.6	1.5	1.7	1.6	1.8	1.7	2.0	1.8	2.1	2.0	2.3	2.1	2.4	2.3
112	1.6	1.4	1.6	1.5	1.8	1.6	1.9	1.7	2.0	1.8	2.1	2.0	2.3	2.1
114	1.5	1.4	1.6	1.4	1.7	1.5	1.8	1.6	1.9	1.7	2.0	1.8	2.1	1.9
116	1.4	1.3	1.5	1.4	1.6	1.4	1.7	1.5	1.8	1.6	1.9	1.7	2.0	1.8
118	1.4	1.2	1.4	1.3	1.5	1.3	1.6	1.4	1.7	1.5	1.8	1.6	1.9	1.7
120	1.3	1.2	1.4	1.2	1.5	1.3	1.5	1.3	1.6	1.4	1.7	1.5	1.8	1.5
122	1.3	1.1	1.4	1.1	1.4	1.2	1.5	1.2	1.5	1.3	1.6	1.4	1.7	1.4
124	1.2	1.0	1.3	1.1	1.4	1.1	1.4	1.2	1.5	1.2	1.6	1.3	1.6	1.3
126	1.2	1.0	1.3	1.0	1.3	1.1	1.4	1.1	1.4	1.2	1.5	1.3	1.6	1.3
128	1.2	0.9	1.2	1.0	1.3	1.0	1.3	1.0	1.4	1.1	1.4	1.1	1.5	1.2
130	1.2	0.9	1.2	0.9	1.2	1.0	1.3	1.0	1.3	1.0	1.4	1.1	1.4	1.1
132	1.1	0.8	1.2	0.9	1.2	0.9	1.2	1.0	1.3	1.0	1.4	1.0	1.4	1.1
134	1.1	0.8	1.1	0.8	1.2	0.8	1.2	0.9	1.3	0.9	1.3	0.9	1.3	1.0
136	1.1	0.8	1.1	0.8	1.2	0.8	1.2	0.8	1.2	0.8	1.3	0.9	1.3	0.9
138	1.1	0.7	1.1	0.7	1.1	0.8	1.2	0.8	1.2	0.8	1.2	0.8	1.3	0.8
140	1.0	0.7	1.1	0.7	1.1	0.7	1.1	0.7	1.2	0.8	1.2	0.8	1.2	0.8
142	1.0	0.6	1.1	0.6	1.1	0.7	1.1	0.7	1.1	0.7	1.2	0.7	1.2	0.7
144	1.0	0.6	1.0	0.6	1.1	0.6	1.1	0.6	1.1	0.7	1.2	0.7	1.2	0.7
146	1.0	0.6	1.0	0.6	1.0	0.6	1.1	0.6	1.1	0.6	1.1	0.6	1.2	0.6
148	1.0	0.5	1.0	0.5	1.0	0.6	1.1	0.6	1.1	0.6	1.1	0.6	1.1	0.6
150	1.0	0.5	1.0	0.5	1.0	0.5	1.0	0.5	1.1	0.5	1.1	0.5	1.1	0.6
152	1.0	0.5	1.0	0.5	1.0	0.5	1.0	0.5	1.0	0.5	1.1	0.5	1.1	0.5
154	1.0	0.4	1.0	0.4	1.0	0.4	1.0	0.4	1.0	0.5	1.1	0.5	1.1	0.5
156	1.0	0.4	1.0	0.4	1.0	0.4	1.0	0.4	1.0	0.4	1.0	0.4	1.1	0.4
158	1.0	0.4	1.0	0.4	1.0	0.4	1.0	0.4	1.0	0.4	1.0	0.4	1.0	0.4
160	1.0	0.3	1.0	0.3	1.0	0.3	1.0	0.3	1.0	0.4	1.0	0.4	1.0	0.4

Difference between course and 2nd bearing

Continued

DISTANCE OF AN OBJECT DETERMINED BY TWO BEARINGS

Difference between course and first bearing

	88°		90°		92°		94°		96°		98°		100°	
98°	5.8	5.7												
100	4.8	4.7	5.8	5.7										
102	4.1	4.0	4.8	4.7	5.8	5.6								
104	3.6	3.5	4.1	4.0	4.8	4.7	5.7	5.6						
106	3.2	3.1	3.6	3.5	4.1	4.0	4.8	4.6	5.7	5.5				
108	2.9	2.8	3.2	3.1	3.6	3.4	4.1	3.9	4.8	4.6	5.7	5.4		
110	2.7	2.5	2.9	2.8	3.2	3.0	3.6	3.4	4.1	3.9	4.8	4.5	5.7	5.3
112	2.5	2.3	2.7	2.5	2.9	2.7	3.2	3.0	3.6	3.4	4.1	3.8	4.7	4.4
114	2.3	2.1	2.5	2.2	2.7	2.4	2.9	2.7	3.2	2.9	3.6	3.3	4.1	3.7
116	2.1	1.9	2.3	2.0	2.5	2.2	2.7	2.4	2.9	2.6	3.2	2.9	3.6	3.2
118	2.0	1.8	2.1	1.9	2.3	2.0	2.4	2.2	2.6	2.3	2.9	2.6	3.2	2.8
120	1.9	1.6	2.0	1.7	2.1	1.8	2.3	2.0	2.4	2.1	2.6	2.3	2.9	2.5
122	1.8	1.5	1.9	1.6	2.0	1.7	2.1	1.8	2.3	1.9	2.4	2.1	2.6	2.2
124	1.7	1.4	1.8	1.5	1.9	1.6	2.0	1.6	2.1	1.8	2.3	1.9	2.4	2.0
126	1.6	1.3	1.7	1.4	1.8	1.4	1.9	1.5	2.0	1.6	2.1	1.7	2.2	1.8
128	1.6	1.2	1.6	1.3	1.7	1.3	1.8	1.4	1.9	1.5	2.0	1.6	2.1	1.6
130	1.5	1.1	1.6	1.2	1.6	1.2	1.7	1.3	1.8	1.4	1.9	1.4	2.0	1.5
132	1.4	1.1	1.5	1.1	1.6	1.2	1.6	1.2	1.7	1.3	1.8	1.3	1.9	1.4
134	1.4	1.0	1.4	1.0	1.5	1.1	1.6	1.1	1.6	1.2	1.7	1.2	1.8	1.3
136	1.3	0.9	1.4	1.0	1.4	1.0	1.5	1.0	1.6	1.1	1.6	1.1	1.7	1.2
138	1.3	0.9	1.4	0.9	1.4	0.9	1.4	1.0	1.5	1.0	1.5	1.0	1.6	1.1
140	1.3	0.8	1.3	0.8	1.3	0.9	1.4	0.9	1.4	0.9	1.5	1.0	1.5	1.0
142	1.2	0.8	1.3	0.8	1.3	0.8	1.3	0.8	1.4	0.8	1.4	0.9	1.5	0.9
144	1.2	0.7	1.2	0.7	1.3	0.8	1.3	0.8	1.3	0.8	1.4	0.8	1.4	0.8
146	1.2	0.7	1.2	0.7	1.2	0.7	1.3	0.7	1.3	0.7	1.3	0.8	1.4	0.7
148	1.2	0.6	1.2	0.6	1.2	0.6	1.2	0.6	1.3	0.7	1.3	0.7	1.3	0.7
150	1.1	0.6	1.2	0.6	1.2	0.6	1.2	0.6	1.2	0.6	1.3	0.6	1.3	0.6
152	1.1	0.5	1.1	0.5	1.2	0.5	1.2	0.6	1.2	0.6	1.2	0.6	1.2	0.6
154	1.1	0.5	1.1	0.5	1.1	0.5	1.2	0.5	1.2	0.5	1.2	0.5	1.2	0.5
156	1.1	0.4	1.1	0.4	1.1	0.4	1.1	0.5	1.2	0.5	1.2	0.5	1.2	0.5
158	1.1	0.4	1.1	0.4	1.1	0.4	1.1	0.4	1.1	0.4	1.1	0.4	1.2	0.4
160	1.0	0.4	1.1	0.4	1.1	0.4	1.1	0.4	1.1	0.4	1.1	0.4	1.1	0.4

Difference between course and 2nd bearing

Continued

64

DISTANCE OF AN OBJECT DETERMINED BY TWO BEARINGS

Difference between course and first bearing

	102°	104°	106°	108°	110°	112°	114°
112	5.6 5.2						
114	4.7 4.3	5.6 5.1					
116	4.0 3.6	4.7 4.2	5.5 5.0				
118	3.6 3.1	4.0 3.5	4.6 4.1	5.5 4.8			
120	3.2 2.7	3.5 3.0	4.0 3.4	4.6 4.0	5.4 4.7		
122	2.9 2.4	3.1 2.7	3.5 3.0	3.9 3.3	4.5 3.8	5.3 4.5	
124	2.6 2.2	2.8 2.4	3.1 2.6	3.4 2.9	3.9 3.2	4.5 3.7	5.3 4.4
126	2.4 2.0	2.6 2.1	2.8 2.3	3.1 2.5	3.4 2.8	3.8 3.1	4.4 3.6
128	2.2 1.8	2.4 1.9	2.6 2.0	2.8 2.2	3.0 2.4	3.4 2.6	3.8 3.0
130	2.1 1.6	2.2 1.7	2.4 1.8	2.5 1.9	2.8 2.1	3.0 2.3	3.3 2.5
132	2.0 1.4	2.1 1.5	2.2 1.6	2.3 1.7	2.5 1.9	2.7 2.0	3.0 2.2
134	1.8 1.3	1.9 1.4	2.0 1.5	2.2 1.6	2.3 1.7	2.5 1.8	2.7 1.9
136	1.8 1.2	1.8 1.3	1.9 1.3	2.0 1.4	2.1 1.5	2.3 1.6	2.4 1.7
138	1.7 1.1	1.7 1.2	1.8 1.2	1.9 1.3	2.0 1.3	2.1 1.4	2.2 1.5
140	1.6 1.0	1.6 1.1	1.7 1.1	1.8 1.2	1.9 1.2	2.0 1.3	2.1 1.3
142	1.5 0.9	1.6 1.0	1.6 1.0	1.7 1.0	1.8 1.1	1.8 1.1	2.0 1.2
144	1.5 0.9	1.5 0.9	1.6 0.9	1.6 1.0	1.7 1.0	1.8 1.0	1.8 1.1
146	1.4 0.8	1.4 0.8	1.5 0.8	1.5 0.9	1.6 0.9	1.7 0.9	1.7 1.0
148	1.4 0.7	1.4 0.7	1.4 0.8	1.5 0.8	1.5 0.8	1.6 0.8	1.6 0.9
150	1.3 0.7	1.4 0.7	1.4 0.7	1.4 0.7	1.5 0.7	1.5 0.8	1.6 0.8
152	1.3 0.6	1.3 0.6	1.3 0.6	1.4 0.6	1.4 0.7	1.4 0.7	1.5 0.7
154	1.2 0.5	1.3 0.6	1.3 0.6	1.3 0.6	1.4 0.6	1.4 0.6	1.4 0.6
156	1.2 0.5	1.2 0.5	1.2 0.5	1.3 0.5	1.3 0.5	1.3 0.5	1.4 0.6
158	1.2 0.4	1.2 0.4	1.2 0.5	1.2 0.5	1.3 0.5	1.3 0.5	1.3 0.5
160	1.2 0.4	1.2 0.4	1.2 0.4	1.2 0.4	1.2 0.4	1.2 0.4	1.3 0.4

	116°	118°	120°	122°	124°	126°	128°
126	5.2 4.2						
128	4.3 3.4	5.1 4.0					
130	3.7 2.8	4.2 3.2	5.0 3.8				
132	3.3 2.4	3.6 2.7	4.2 3.1	4.9 3.6			
134	2.9 2.1	3.2 2.3	3.6 2.6	4.1 2.9	4.8 3.4		
136	2.6 1.8	2.9 2.0	3.1 2.2	3.5 2.4	4.0 2.8	4.7 3.2	
138	2.4 1.6	2.6 1.7	2.8 1.9	3.1 2.1	3.4 2.3	3.9 2.6	4.5 3.0
140	2.2 1.4	2.4 1.5	2.5 1.6	2.7 1.8	3.0 1.9	3.3 2.2	3.8 2.4
142	2.0 1.3	2.2 1.3	2.3 1.4	2.5 1.5	2.7 1.6	2.9 1.8	3.3 2.0
144	1.9 1.1	2.0 1.2	2.1 1.2	2.3 1.3	2.4 1.4	2.6 1.5	2.9 1.7
146	1.8 1.0	1.9 1.0	2.0 1.1	2.1 1.2	2.2 1.2	2.4 1.3	2.6 1.4
148	1.7 0.9	1.8 0.9	1.8 1.0	1.9 1.0	2.0 1.1	2.2 1.1	2.3 1.2
150	1.6 0.8	1.7 0.8	1.7 0.9	1.8 0.9	1.9 1.0	2.0 1.0	2.1 1.0
152	1.5 0.7	1.6 0.7	1.6 0.8	1.7 0.8	1.8 0.8	1.8 0.9	1.9 0.9
154	1.5 0.6	1.5 0.7	1.6 0.7	1.6 0.7	1.7 0.7	1.7 0.8	1.8 0.8
156	1.4 0.6	1.4 0.6	1.5 0.6	1.5 0.6	1.6 0.6	1.6 0.7	1.7 0.7
158	1.3 0.5	1.4 0.5	1.4 0.5	1.4 0.5	1.5 0.6	1.5 0.6	1.6 0.6
160	1.3 0.4	1.3 0.4	1.4 0.5	1.4 0.5	1.4 0.5	1.4 0.5	1.5 0.5

	130°	132°	134°	136°	138°	140°	142°
140	4.4 2.8						
142	3.7 2.3	4.3 2.6					
144	3.2 1.9	3.6 2.1	4.1 2.4				
146	2.8 1.6	3.1 1.7	3.5 1.9	4.0 2.2			
148	2.5 1.3	2.7 1.4	3.0 1.6	3.3 1.8	3.8 2.0		
150	2.2 1.1	2.4 1.2	2.6 1.3	2.9 1.4	3.2 1.6	3.7 1.8	
152	2.0 1.0	2.2 1.0	2.3 1.1	2.5 1.2	2.8 1.3	3.1 1.4	3.6 1.7
154	1.9 0.8	2.0 0.9	2.1 0.9	2.2 1.0	2.4 1.1	2.7 1.2	3.0 1.3
156	1.8 0.7	1.8 0.7	1.9 0.8	2.0 0.8	2.2 0.9	2.3 1.0	2.5 1.0
158	1.6 0.6	1.7 0.6	1.8 0.7	1.8 0.7	2.0 0.7	2.1 0.8	2.2 0.8
160	1.5 0.5	1.6 0.5	1.6 0.6	1.7 0.6	1.8 0.6	1.9 0.6	2.0 0.7

Difference between course and 2nd bearing

Distance of an Object by Two Bearings: Quick Solutions

In addition to the tabular method for finding distances off by two bearings and the run between, there are several special cases where shortcut solutions are possible without the use of tables. It is still necessary, however, to have an adequate sighting compass and an accurate notion of the boat's speed.

Bow and beam bearing: This method simply puts to use the fact that the two short sides of a right triangle are the same length when the angle between each side and the hypotenuse is 45°. Take the first bearing when the mark is 45° off the bow, making careful notes of time and boat speed. Maintaining course and speed, take the second bearing as the mark comes amidships, bearing 90° to the boat's centerline. The distance the boat has traveled between the two bearings will equal the distance of the boat from the mark at the time of the second bearing.

Doubling the angle on the bow: With the boat maintaining course and speed, two bearings are taken on the same object in such a way that the second bearing is twice the relative angle of the first. The distance run between bearings will equal the distance between the second bearing and the object. For example, a boat on a course of 095° is proceeding at 10 knots. At 1010 the skipper takes a bearing on a tower ashore that is 135°, or 40° relative to the vessel. At 1025, the bearing is 175°, or 80° relative to the boat's course. The distance run at 10 knots in 15 minutes is 2.5 nautical miles. The object ashore is thus 2.5 miles from the vessel at the time of the second bearing.

The 7/8 and 7/10 rule: If the first bearing is 22.5° off the bow and the second is 45° off the bow (both relative), then the distance off at the time of the second bearing is the same as the distance run between bearings, **and** the object will be at a distance, when abeam, that is 7/10 the distance of the run between bearings. If the first angle is 30° and the second is 60° (again, both relative), then the distance of the sighted object will be 7/8 the distance run between bearings, when it comes abeam.

Other useful bearing combinations: The following pairs of bearings offer the useful advantages, for the pilot, of knowing in advance his ship's distance off a sighted object. In each case, the run between the two bearings will equal the distance off the object when abeam. Thus, if the first bearing is 22° and the second is 34°, while the run between is two miles, the pilot knows that the sighted object will be two miles off when it comes abeam, assuming he holds his course.

First Bearing	Second Bearing
22°	34°
27°	46°
29°	51°
32°	59°
40°	79°
44°	88°
45°	90°

5/ TIDAL CURRENTS AND TIDAL HEIGHTS

In part, perhaps, because the government publishes annual tables of tides and tidal currents in book form, many otherwise suspicious mariners come to believe in tabulated times of tides and currents as if they were as reliable as the almanac's data on the rising and setting of the sun. The systems included in this chapter for estimating the precise times, heights, and strengths of these phenomena may reinforce that belief, but it's important for the cruising sailor to remember that the material in the NOAA tables, and in this chapter, constitutes nothing more than predictions.

The forecast times, heights, and strengths are carefully calculated, to be sure, and the data are based on vast accumulations of experience. But a strong wind blowing against the prevailing current direction for a few hours can throw off all the tables a good deal. Perhaps the best strategy for the skipper who depends on tidal heights and current strengths is to use these formulas carefully, but with suspicion. If you need to arrive somewhere in time for a particular tide change, arrive early. If you are counting on a predicted current strength, allow some leeway in planning. Then, when predicted tides or currents fail to materialize exactly, you won't be hopelessly fouled up. And on the normal occasions, when matters turn out as predicted, you can take full advantage of the last favoring knot or inch of water.

VELOCITY OF CURRENT AT ANY TIME

From the **Tidal Current Tables** obtain the predicted times of slack water and maximum current bracketing the time for which the velocity is desired, and the velocity of maximum current. Now find the interval of time between slack and the maximum current, and enter the top of one of the two tables below with the interval closest to that value. Find the interval between slack and the time for which the velocity is desired, and enter the side of the table with the interval most nearly corresponding to this value. The intersection of the chosen line and column will be a numerical factor of 1.0 or less. Multiply the maximum velocity of the current by this factor to obtain the approximate velocity at the time desired.

For all **Atlantic Coast (and Gulf Coast) stations** except those in accompanying table.

Interval between slack and maximum current

	1:20	1:40	2:00	2:20	2:40	3:00	3:20	3:40	4:00	4:20	4:40	5:00	5:20	5:40
0:20	0.4	0.3	0.3	0.2	0.2	0.2	0.2	0.1	0.1	0.1	0.1	0.1	0.1	0.1
0:40	0.7	0.6	0.5	0.4	0.4	0.3	0.3	0.3	0.3	0.2	0.2	0.2	0.2	0.2
1:00	0.9	0.8	0.7	0.6	0.6	0.5	0.5	0.4	0.4	0.4	0.3	0.3	0.3	0.3
1:20	1.0	1.0	0.8	0.7	0.6	0.6	0.5	0.5	0.5	0.4	0.4	0.4	0.4	0.4
1:40		1.0	1.0	0.9	0.8	0.8	0.7	0.7	0.6	0.6	0.5	0.5	0.5	0.4
2:00			1.0	1.0	0.9	0.9	0.8	0.8	0.7	0.7	0.6	0.6	0.6	0.5
2:20				1.0	1.0	0.9	0.9	0.8	0.8	0.7	0.7	0.7	0.6	0.6
2:40					1.0	1.0	1.0	0.9	0.9	0.8	0.8	0.7	0.7	0.7
3:00						1.0	1.0	1.0	0.9	0.9	0.8	0.8	0.8	0.7
3:20							1.0	1.0	1.0	0.9	0.9	0.9	0.8	0.8
3:40								1.0	1.0	1.0	0.9	0.9	0.9	0.9
4:00									1.0	1.0	1.0	1.0	0.9	0.9
4:20										1.0	1.0	1.0	1.0	0.9
4:40											1.0	1.0	1.0	1.0
5:00												1.0	1.0	1.0
5:20													1.0	1.0
5:40														1.0

Interval between slack water and desired time

For **Cape Cod Canal, Hell Gate, Chesapeake & Delaware Canal, and all subordinate stations** referred to them.

Interval between slack and maximum current

	1:20	1:40	2:00	2:20	2:40	3:00	3:20	3:40	4:00	4:20	4:40	5:00	5:20	5:40
0:20	0.5	0.4	0.4	0.3	0.3	0.3	0.3	0.3	0.2	0.2	0.2	0.2	0.2	0.2
0:40	0.8	0.7	0.6	0.5	0.5	0.5	0.4	0.4	0.4	0.4	0.3	0.3	0.3	0.3
1:00	0.9	0.8	0.8	0.7	0.7	0.6	0.6	0.5	0.5	0.5	0.4	0.4	0.4	0.4
1:20	1.0	1.0	0.9	0.8	0.8	0.7	0.7	0.6	0.6	0.6	0.5	0.5	0.5	0.5
1:40		1.0	1.0	0.9	0.9	0.8	0.8	0.7	0.7	0.7	0.6	0.6	0.6	0.6
2:00			1.0	1.0	0.9	0.9	0.9	0.8	0.8	0.7	0.7	0.7	0.7	0.6
2:20				1.0	1.0	1.0	0.9	0.9	0.8	0.8	0.8	0.7	0.7	0.7
2:40					1.0	1.0	1.0	0.9	0.9	0.9	0.8	0.8	0.8	0.7
3:00						1.0	1.0	1.0	0.9	0.9	0.9	0.9	0.8	0.8
3:20							1.0	1.0	1.0	1.0	0.9	0.9	0.9	0.8
3:40								1.0	1.0	1.0	1.0	0.9	0.9	0.9
4:00									1.0	1.0	1.0	1.0	0.9	0.9
4:20										1.0	1.0	1.0	1.0	0.9
4:40											1.0	1.0	1.0	1.0
5:00												1.0	1.0	1.0
5:20													1.0	1.0
5:40														1.0

Interval between slack water and desired time

Example: Using the first of the two tables opposite, find the approximate velocity of the current in The Race, Long Island Sound at 1415 on August 7. If you inspected the daily current predictions, you would see that the nearest slack water is at 1229, and the maximum ebb velocity (4.8 knots) is at 1557. The interval between slack and maximum current is thus 3 hours 28 minutes, so you enter the top of the table at 3:20, the closest designated value. The interval between slack water and the desired time is 1 hour 46 minutes, so you enter the side of the table at 1:40. The intersection of the line and column is a factor of 0.7. Multiplying this factor by the maximum velocity of the current gives you a current of 3.4 knots, ebbing. (Note: We're assuming that all the times referred to are Standard Time, as are the times in both the **Tide Tables** and **Tidal Current Tables**.)

Velocity of Current at Subordinate Station

To find the current velocity for a subordinate station, the procedure to be used is not unlike that for finding the height of the tide at an intermediate point. The completed form below will help guide you through the procedure. In addition, several blank forms have been provided; one accompanies this chapter, where it appears with a similar form for tidal height calculations, and the others appear in Appendix B.

To use the form, determine the reference station on which predictions for the subordinate station are based. Fill in the times of slack water and maximum current bracketing the time desired, as well as the velocity of maximum current. In column 2, write down the local differences for your subordinate station (from Table 2 of the **Tidal Current Tables**). These differences will include times of slack and maximum current and the ratio of the current velocity at the subordinate station to that at the reference station.

Use these values to complete column 3, and in the next column, enter the time difference between slack and maximum current at the subordinate station. The rest of the procedure is exactly like the one already introduced for a reference station.

CURRENT AT ANY TIME, SUBORDINATE STATION	Place __Bay Shore__ Time __1315__ Date __7/28__						
Reference Station:	Table 2 Differences		Local Current		Interval Slack/Max	Interval Slack/Time	Corr'n Factor 0.8
Time vel	h. m.	v. r.	time vel		h. m.	h. m.	
Slack 0849	+2:23		1112		3:34	2:03	Current Velocity 2.4
Max 1207 3.75	+2:39	0.8	1446 3.0				
Ebb/Flood							

69

HEIGHT OF TIDE AT SUBORDINATE STATION

HEIGHT AT ANY TIME   Place_____

                            Time _____Date_____

Reference Station:	Table 2 Differences			Time	Local Height	Tidal Data Duration	Range	Time from High/Low	Corr'n factor
time ht.	h.	m.	ft.			h. m.	ft.	h. m.	
High									
Low									Ht. of tide
High									Corr'n factor
Low									Ht. of tide
High									Corr'n factor
Low									Ht. of tide

VELOCITY OF CURRENT AT SUBORDINATE STATION

CURRENT AT ANY TIME   Place_____

                            Time_____ Date_____

	Reference Station	Table 2 Differences			Local Current		Interval Slack/Max	Interval Slack/Time	
	Time vel.	h. m.	v. r.	time	vel.	h. m.	h. m.		
Slack									Corr'n Factor
Max	Ebb/Flood								Current Velocity
Slack									Corr'n Factor
Max	Ebb/Flood								Current Velocity
Slack									Corr'n Factor
Max	Ebb/Flood								Current Velocity

DURATION OF SLACK WATER

True slack water — high or low — is a term of convenience, indicating the instant when the tidal current is not moving at all. For all practical purposes, however, there is a period of near-zero current either side of slack, a period that decreases in length as the maximum current increases in velocity.

The tables below show the approximate length of time when, for tidal currents of varying maximum strengths, the current will be relatively weak — from below 0.1 up to 0.5 knot. This period encompasses the end of the flood or ebb (as the case may be) and the beginning of the following ebb or flood, and will be spaced evenly on either side of the moment of slack water. That is, if high slack at a point is at 0730, and the maximum current at that point is 3.4 knots, then there will be a period of approximately 34 minutes, from 0713 to 0747, when the current will be 0.5 knot or less.

For areas where there is a difference between the maximum flood and ebb velocities, calculate hypothetical periods of weak current for each velocity and average the two. **Example:** The maximum ebb velocity at an inlet is 4.5 knots, and the maximum flood velocity is 3.5 knots. The duration of current velocity less than 0.5 knot will be the average of 34.5 and 26, or a bit over 30 minutes.

For all Atlantic Coast (and Gulf Coast) stations except those in the accompanying table.

Maximum current Knots	Period with a velocity not more than:				
	0.1 knot	0.2 knot	0.3 knot	0.4 knot	0.5 knot
	Minutes	Minutes	Minutes	Minutes	Minutes
1.0	23	46	70	94	120
1.5	15	31	46	62	78
2.0	11	23	35	46	58
3.0	8	15	23	31	38
4.0	6	11	17	23	29
5.0	5	9	14	18	23
6.0	4	8	11	15	19
7.0	3	7	10	13	16
8.0	3	6	9	11	14
9.0	3	5	8	10	13
10.0	2	5	7	9	11

For Cape Cod Canal, Hell Gate, Chesapeake & Delaware Canal, and all subordinate stations referred to them.

Maximum current Knots	Period with a velocity not more than:				
	0.1 knot	0.2 knot	0.3 knot	0.4 knot	0.5 knot
	Minutes	Minutes	Minutes	Minutes	Minutes
1.0	13	28	46	66	89
1.5	8	18	28	39	52
2.0	6	13	20	28	36
3.0	4	8	13	18	22
4.0	3	6	9	13	17
5.0	3	5	8	10	13

HEIGHT OF TIDE AT ANY TIME

Tables XIX and XX enable you to calculate in advance the height of tide at any time, either for the reference stations in the **Tide Tables** or for the subordinate stations listed in the same volume under Table 2, Tidal Differences. Before using the tables, be sure to convert the times of interest, if necessary, to Standard Time, since this is the time used in the **Tide Tables.** From the **Tide Tables** read the times of the high and low waters that bracket the time of immediate interest on the appropriate date; the interval between these is the **duration of rise or fall.** The difference between the high and low water heights is the **tidal range.**

Enter the left-hand column of Table XIX with the calculated duration of rise or fall, and find there the value that most nearly agrees. On the corresponding horizontal line, locate the value that best approximates the actual time differential from the nearest high or low water to the time of interest.

Using that value as a starting point, drop directly down to Table XX — this locates you in the proper column. In the left-hand column of Table XX find the value that most nearly approaches the tidal range of interest. Where the corresponding line intersects the previously located column, a correction factor will be found. When the nearest stand is high water, subtract the correction factor from the high water height; conversely, when the nearest stand is low water, add the correction to the low water height.

Example: You need to know the height of tide at Newport, Rhode Island, at 1800 on July 23. You consult the **Tide Tables** and discover that low water is − 0.1 foot at 1507 and high water is 3.9 feet at 2140. The duration of rise is thus 6 hours 33 minutes, and the tidal range is 4.0 feet. The nearest stand is low water, 2 hours 53 minutes before your selected time.

Entering the upper half of the table at 6 hours 40 minutes, move to the third column from the right, 2 hours 53 minutes. Dropping straight down to Table XX, on the line corresponding to a tidal range of 4.0 feet, you'll find a corrrection factor of 1.6. Since the nearest tide is low, add 1.6 to −0.1: the tide at Newport at 1800 will be 1.5 feet above the datum of soundings, which in this case is Mean Low Water. (On new charts, datum is being changed to Mean Lower Low Water, but it will be some years before this is reflected in all Atlantic and Gulf Coast charts.)

Example: Given a high water at Seattle, Washington, of 8.8 feet, at 1349 on April 20, you need to know the height of the tide at 1500. The next low water is at 2009, and its height is 1.2 feet. You thus calculate that the duration of fall is 6 hours 20 minutes, and the range is 7.6 feet. The nearest turning point is high water, 1 hour 11 minutes before your selected time.

Enter Table XIX at 6 hours 20 minutes and move to the sixth column from the left, since 1 hour 16 minutes is closest to 1 hour 11 minutes.

Directly below in Table XX, on the line corresponding to a tidal range of 7.5 feet, is the correction factor, 0.7. Since the nearest stand is high, subtract 0.7 from the high water height, 8.8. At 1500 on April 20, therefore, the tide at the reference station for Seattle will be 8.1 feet above the datum of soundings, which for Seattle is Mean Lower Low Water.

TABLES XIX, XX. HEIGHT OF TIDE AT ANY TIME

Duration-Rise/Fall H. M.	Time from the nearest high or low water														
	H.M.	H.M.	H.M.	H.M.	H.M.	H.M.	H.M.	H.M.	H.M.	H.M.	H.M.	H.M.	H.M.	H.M.	H.M.
4 00	0 08	0 16	0 24	0 32	0 40	0 48	0 56	1 04	1 12	1 20	1 28	1 36	1 44	1 52	2 00
4 20	0 09	0 17	0 26	0 35	0 43	0 52	1 01	1 09	1 18	1 27	1 35	1 44	1 53	2 01	2 10
4 40	0 09	0 19	0 28	0 37	0 47	0 56	1 05	1 15	1 24	1 33	1 43	1 52	2 01	2 11	2 20
5 00	0 10	0 20	0 30	0 40	0 50	1 00	1 10	1 20	1 30	1 40	1 50	2 00	2 10	2 20	2 30
5 20	0 11	0 21	0 32	0 43	0 53	1 04	1 15	1 25	1 36	1 47	1 57	2 08	2 19	2 29	2 40
5 40	0 11	0 23	0 34	0 45	0 57	1 08	1 19	1 31	1 42	1 53	2 05	2 16	2 27	2 39	2 50
6 00	0 12	0 24	0 36	0 48	1 00	1 12	1 24	1 36	1 48	2 00	2 12	2 24	2 36	2 48	3 00
6 20	0 13	0 25	0 38	0 51	1 03	1 16	1 29	1 41	1 54	2 07	2 19	2 32	2 45	2 57	3 10
6 40	0 13	0 27	0 40	0 53	1 07	1 20	1 33	1 47	2 00	2 13	2 27	2 40	2 53	3 07	3 20
7 00	0 14	0 28	0 42	0 56	1 10	1 24	1 38	1 52	2 06	2 20	2 34	2 48	3 02	3 16	3 30
7 20	0 15	0 29	0 44	0 59	1 13	1 28	1 43	1 57	2 12	2 27	2 41	2 56	3 11	3 25	3 40
7 40	0 15	0 31	0 46	1 01	1 17	1 32	1 47	2 03	2 18	2 33	2 49	3 04	3 19	3 35	3 50
8 00	0 16	0 32	0 48	1 04	1 20	1 36	1 52	2 08	2 24	2 40	2 56	3 12	3 28	3 44	4 00
8 20	0 17	0 33	0 50	1 07	1 23	1 40	1 57	2 13	2 30	2 47	3 03	3 20	3 37	3 53	4 10
8 40	0 17	0 35	0 52	1 09	1 27	1 44	2 01	2 19	2 36	2 53	3 11	3 28	3 45	4 03	4 20
9 00	0 18	0 36	0 54	1 12	1 30	1 48	2 06	2 24	2 42	3 00	3 18	3 36	3 54	4 12	4 30
9 20	0 19	0 37	0 56	1 15	1 33	1 52	2 11	2 29	2 48	3 07	3 25	3 44	4 03	4 21	4 40
9 40	0 19	0 39	0 58	1 17	1 37	1 56	2 15	2 35	2 54	3 13	3 33	3 52	4 11	4 31	4 50
10 00	0 20	0 40	1 00	1 20	1 40	2 00	2 20	2 40	3 00	3 20	3 40	4 00	4 20	4 40	5 00
10 20	0 21	0 41	1 02	1 23	1 43	2 04	2 25	2 45	3 06	3 27	3 47	4 08	4 29	4 49	5 10
10 40	0 21	0 43	1 04	1 25	1 47	2 00	2 29	2 51	3 12	3 33	3 55	4 16	4 37	4 59	5 20

Range – Ft.	Correction to height														
	Ft.	Ft.	Ft.	Ft.	Ft.	Ft.	Ft.	Ft.	Ft.	Ft.	Ft.	Ft.	Ft.	Ft.	Ft.
0 5	0.0	0.0	0.0	0.0	0.0	0.0	0.1	0.1	0.1	0.1	0.1	0.2	0.2	0.2	0.2
1.0	0.0	0.0	0.0	0.0	0.1	0.1	0.1	0.2	0.2	0.2	0.3	0.3	0.40	0.4	0.5
1.5	0.0	0.0	0.0	0.1	0.1	0.1	0.2	0.2	0.3	0.4	0.4	0.5	0.6	0.7	0.8
2.0	0.0	0.0	0.0	0.1	0.1	0.2	0.3	0.3	0.4	0.5	0.6	0.7	0.8	0.9	1.0
2.5	0.0	0.0	0.0	0.1	0.1	0.2	0.3	0.3	0.4	0.5	0.6	0.7	0.8	0.9	1.0
3.0	0.0	0.0	0.1	0.1	0.2	0.3	0.4	0.5	0.6	0.8	0.9	1.0	1.2	1.3	1.5
3.5	0.0	0.0	0.1	0.2	0.2	0.3	0.4	0.6	0.7	0.9	1.0	1.2	1.4	1.6	1.8
4.0	0.0	0.0	0.1	0.2	0.3	0.4	0.5	0.7	0.8	1.0	1.2	1.4	1.6	1.8	2.0
4.5	0.0	0.0	0.1	0.2	0.3	0.4	0.6	0.7	0.9	1.1	1.3	1.6	1.8	2.0	2.2
5.0	0.0	0.1	0.1	0.2	0.4	0.5	0.7	0.9	1.1	1.4	1.6	1.9	2.2	2.5	2.8
5.5	0.0	0.1	0.1	0.2	0.4	0.5	0.7	0.9	1.1	1.4	1.6	1.9	2.2	2.5	2.8
6.0	0.0	0.1	0.1	0.3	0.4	0.6	0.8	1.0	1.2	1.5	1.8	2.1	2.4	2.7	3.0
6.5	0.0	0.1	0.2	0.3	0.4	0.6	0.8	1.1	1.3	1.6	1.9	2.2	2.6	2.9	3.2
7.0	0.0	0.1	0.2	0.3	0.5	0.7	0.9	1.2	1.4	1.8	2.1	2.4	2.8	3.1	3.5
7.5	0.0	0.1	0.2	0.3	0.5	0.7	1.0	1.2	1.5	1.9	2.2	2.6	3.0	3.4	3.8
8.0	0.0	0.1	0.2	0.3	0.5	0.8	1.0	1.3	1.6	2.0	2.4	2.8	3.2	3.6	4.0
8.5	0.0	0.1	0.2	0.4	0.6	0.8	1.1	1.4	1.8	2.1	2.5	2.9	3.4	3.8	4.2
9.0	0.0	0.1	0.2	0.4	0.6	0.9	1.2	1.5	1.9	2.2	2.7	3.1	3.6	4.0	4.5
9.5	0.0	0.1	0.2	0.4	0.6	0.9	1.2	1.6	2.0	2.4	2.8	3.3	3.8	4.3	4.8
10.0	0.0	0.1	0.2	0.4	0.7	1.0	1.3	1.7	2.1	2.5	3.0	3.5	4.0	4.5	5.0
10.5	0.0	0.1	0.3	0.5	0.7	1.0	1.3	1.7	2.2	2.6	3.1	3.6	4.2	4.7	5.2
11.0	0.0	0.1	0.3	0.5	0.7	1.1	1.4	1.8	2.3	2.8	3.3	3.8	4.4	4.9	5.5
11.5	0.0	0.1	0.3	0.5	0.8	1.1	1.5	1.9	2.4	2.9	3.4	4.0	4.6	5.1	5.8
12.0	0.0	0.1	0.3	0.5	0.8	1.1	1.5	2.0	2.5	3.0	3.6	4.1	4.0	5.4	6.0
12.5	0.0	0.1	0.3	0.5	0.8	1.2	1.6	2.1	2.6	3.1	3.7	4.3	5.0	5.6	6.2
13.0	0.0	0.1	0.3	0.6	0.9	1.2	1.7	2.2	2.7	3.2	3.9	4.5	5.1	5.8	6.5
13.5	0.0	0.1	0.3	0.6	0.9	1.3	1.7	2.2	2.8	3.4	4.0	4.7	5.3	6.0	6.8
14.0	0.0	0.2	0.3	0.6	0.9	1.3	1.8	2.3	2.9	3.5	4.2	4.8	5.5	6.3	7.0
14.5	0.0	0.2	0.4	0.6	1.0	1.4	1.9	2.4	3.0	3.6	4.3	5.0	5.7	6.5	7.2
15.0	0.0	0.2	0.4	0.6	1.0	1.4	1.9	2.5	3.1	3.8	4.4	5.2	5.9	6.7	7.5
15.5	0.0	0.2	0.4	0.7	1.0	1.5	2.0	2.6	3.2	3.9	4.6	5.4	6.1	6.9	7.8
16.0	0.0	0.2	0.4	0.7	1.1	1.5	2.1	2.6	3.3	4.0	4.7	5.5	6.3	7.2	8.0
16.5	0.0	0.2	0.4	0.7	1.1	1.6	2.1	2.7	3.4	4.1	4.9	5.7	6.5	7.4	8.2
17.0	0.0	0.2	0.4	0.7	1.1	1.6	2.2	2.8	3.5	4.2	5.0	5.9	6.7	7.6	8.5
17.5	0.0	0.2	0.4	0.8	1.2	1.7	2.2	2.9	3.6	4.4	5.2	6.0	6.9	7.8	8.8
18.0	0.0	0.2	0.4	0.8	1.2	1.7	2.3	3.0	3.7	4.5	5.3	6.2	7.1	8.1	9.0
18.5	0.1	0.2	0.5	0.8	1.2	1.8	2.4	3.1	3.8	4.6	5.5	6.4	7.3	8.3	9.2
19.0	0.1	0.2	0.5	0.8	1.3	1.8	2.4	3.1	3.9	4.8	5.6	6.6	7.5	8.5	9.5
19.5	0.1	0.2	0.5	0.8	1.3	1.9	2.5	3.2	4.0	4.9	5.8	6.7	7.7	8.7	9.8
20.0	0.1	0.2	0.5	0.9	1.3	1.9	2.6	3.3	4.1	5.0	5.9	6.9	7.9	9.0	10.0

Height of Tide at Subordinate Station

Only a small amount of extra work is necessary to predict the height of tide at any time for a subordinate station. Remember, however, that any estimate of tidal height or current is precisely that — an estimate. Under normal conditions the estimate should be good, but unusual winds or seas can have a marked effect both on times of high and low water and on tidal heights. For this reason, it's often a good idea, when a voyage brings you near an operative tide gauge (almost every bridge and many marinas have one), to compare a predicted tidal height to the actual height. If the prediction is way off, probably the current prediction will be off, too.

Example: You're approaching South Dartmouth, Massachusetts, off Buzzards Bay, and you want to know the state of the tide there at 1800 on September 8. First check Table 2 of the **Tide Tables** to find the reference station for South Dartmouth (it happens to be Newport, Rhode Island), then note the several differences on the Newport tidal predictions: high water at South Dartmouth is +0 hours 28 minutes on Newport (i.e., 28 minutes later than Newport); low water is +0 hours 38 minutes; high water at South Dartmouth is predicted to be 0.2 foot higher than at Newport for any given day; low water is 0.0 on Newport, that is, the same height.

You can then calculate the predicted state of the tide at South Dartmouth. The form below has been completed to help guide you through the procedure. Several additional blank forms have been provided; one accompanies this chapter, where it appears with a similar form for tidal current calculations, and the others appear in Appendix B.

First, look up the data for the high and low water at Newport on September 8 that bracket your desired time, 1800. In this case they are: high water 2332, height 3.5; low water 1654, height −0.2. Now fill in the first two columns of the form, as shown. It's a wise idea to put plus or minus signs before all heights and before the time differences applied to the reference station data. Next, using the information thus recorded, complete the rest of the form over to the right-hand column. To obtain the correction factor and the predicted tidal height, use Tables XIX and XX exactly as previously described for a reference station.

TIDE AT GIVEN TIME, SUBORDINATE STATION	Place: _South Dartmouth, Mass._ Time: _1800_ Date: _9/8_								
	Reference Station:		Table 2 Differences		Time	Local Height	Tidal Data Duration h. m.	Range ft.	Time from High/Low h. m.	Corr'n factor
	time	ht.	h. m.	ft.						0.0
High	2332	+3.5	+0:28	+0.2	0000	+3.7	6:28	3.9	0:28	Ht. of tide
Low	1654	−0.2	+0:38	0.0	1732	−0.2				−0.2

6/ **PLOTTING AND CHARTING**

Good publications are essential if the pilot is to lay off his courses with any kind of confidence. But like anything else worthwhile, charts, tide tables, and cruising guides cost money. Unlike some other publications, the navigator's tend to become obsolete rather quickly.

Everyone has his own opinion concerning the frequency with which a skipper should invest in new charts. Everyone but me, that is, because I don't really know — it depends too much on variables. My only personal rule is that I should always get brand-new charts for a major cruise to an area I'm unfamiliar with. Charts of my own locale I keep largely as memory aids. Chart stowage is another problem, especially in smaller boats. Someday I hope to have a really good chart table that will include the following features: (1) flat stowage, without folding or rolling, for the largest charts; (2) secure yet accessible niches for pencils, protractors, dividers, etc.; (3) repeater dials for the speedometer, depth sounder, anemometer, and apparent wind gauge; (4) fingertip access to the ship's RDF, Loran receiver, and radio transmitter; (5) access to the cockpit. More and more U.S.-built boats are turning up with adequate arrangements for the pilot, but there are still far too many so-called cruising boats in which the unfortunate navigator has to share his space with the cook or the people eating their supper. In the absence of a proper permanent chart table, a good (and expensive) wooden chart case is probably the next best thing.

Plotting, as someone once told me, is apt to be rather quixotic on a small cruiser. Answers to tenths of a mile might be scribbled hopefully on soggy paper, while the whole conveyance leaps about like a pea on a drumhead.

How accurate can one be under those circumstances? In truth, pinpoint accuracy is not always feasible, but there is something to be said for arriving at the most precise answer possible, plotting it as carefully as one can, then steering the boat with reasonable precision. It all boils down to a resolve not to round off too early in the game.

Another important thing, I think, is to keep the plot up-to-the-minute (well, up-to-the-hour, actually). Frequent plotting will polish your skills and will also minimize the chances of becoming positionally disoriented (or, as we navigators say, "lost").

Finally, once you've arrived at the best possible answer, use it. Don't try to second-guess your plotting unless you receive new information. As a general rule, work done in tranquility is more reliable than a hunch; at worst, it is usually easier to figure out where you went wrong in a piloting problem if you follow your solution — erroneous though it be — than if you begin fiddling with it.

TABLE XXI. CHART ABBREVIATIONS.

Italicized lettering on the chart (bold lettering here) indicates water, underwater, and floating features. Regular lettering indicates features that are dry at high water and are not affected by movement of the water. For a more complete index to lettering styles, see the National Ocean Survey's Chart No. 1.

1. Coast features

Anch	Anchorage	**Pass**	Passage
Apprs	Approaches	Pen	Peninsula
Arch	Archipelago	Pk	Peak
B	Bay, Bayou	Prom	Promontory
Bld	Boulder	Pt	Point
C	Cove	**R**	River
C	Cape	Rd	Road, Roadstead
Chan	Channel	Rg	Range
Cr	Creek	**Rk**	Rock, covered at high tide
Entr	Entrance	Rk	Rock, above water at high tide
Est	Estuary		
Fd	Fjord	**Rky**	Rocky
G	Gulf	**Sd**	Sound
Hbr	Harbor	**Slu**	Slough
Hd	Head, Headland	**Str**	Strait, Stream
Hn	Haven	Sw	Swamp
I	Island	**Thoro**	Thorofare
In	Inlet	Vol	Volcano
Is	Islands		
It	Islet		
L	Lake, Lough		
Lag	Lagoon	**2. Adjectives, Adverbs, etc.**	
Ldg	Landing		
Ma	Marsh	aband	Abandoned
Mg	Mangrove	abt	About
Mt	Mountain	AERO	Aeronautical
Mth	Mouth	anc	Ancient
P	Port, Pond	AUTH	Authorized

CL	Clearance
concr	Concrete
conspic	Conspicuous
cor	Corner
D, Destr	Destroyed
DD	Deep draft
discontd	Discontinued
dist	Distant
E'ly	Easterly
elec	Electrical
estab	Established
exper	Experimental
explos	Explosive
extr	Extreme
fl	Flood
gt	Great
LNM	Local Notice to Mariners
lit	Little
Lrg	Large
maintd	Maintained
max	Maximum
mid	Middle
min	Minimum
mod	Moderate
NM	Notice to Mariners
N'ly	Northerly
occas	Occasional
priv	Private
prohib	Prohibited
prom	Prominent
Restr	Restricted
S'ly	Southerly
sk	Stroke
sml	Small
St	Saint
std	Standard
subb	Submarine
subm	Submerged
temp	Temporary
unverd	Unverified
W'ly	Westerly

3. Buildings and Structures

ABAND LT HO	Abandoned Lighthouse
Cath	Cathedral
Chy	Chimney, Stack
Ct Ho	Courthouse
Cup	Cupola
Cus Ho	Customs House
Facty	Factory
FP	Flagpole
FS	Flagstaff

Gab	Gable
Hosp	Hospital
HS	High School
LOOK TR	Watch tower
Mon	Monument
Pav	Pavilion
PO	Post Office
Ru	Ruins
Sch	School
S'pipe	Water tower, Standpipe
Tel Off	Telegraph Office
T	Telephone
Tk	Tank
Tr	Tower
Univ	University

4. Colors of Lights

Am	Amber
B	Blue
G	Green
Irreg	Irregular light
Occas	Occasional light
Or	Orange
R	Red
Temp	Temporary light
Vi	Violet
W	White
Y	Yellow
RGE	Range
TLB	Temporary lighted buoy
TRLB	Temporarily replaced by lighted buoy showing same characteristics
TRUB	Temporarily replaced by an unlighted buoy
TUB	Temporary unlighted buoy

5. Buoys and Beacons

Am	Amber
B	Black
Bn	Beacon, in general
Bu	Blue
G	Green
Or	Orange
R	Red
Ra Ref	Radar reflector
W	White
Y	Yellow

6. Radio and Radar Stations

AERO R BN	Aeronautical radio beacon
MICRO TR	Microwave tower
Ra Dome	Radar Dome

Ra Ref	Radar reflector
R Bn	Radiobeacon
R MAST	Radio mast
R TR	Radio tower
TV TR	Television mast or tower

7. Dangers

(25)	Rock that does not cover, height above MHW — 25 feet, in this case
*(2)	Rock that covers and uncovers, height above chart datum of soundings
+	Submerged rock, depth unknown
Bk	Bank
ED	Existence doubtful
Le	Ledge
PA	Position approximate
PD	Position doubtful
Rf	Reef
SD	Doubtful sounding
Shl	Shoal
Wks	Wreckage

8. Quality of the Bottom

bk	Black
Blds	Boulders
br	Brown
brk	Broken
bu	Blue
Ca	Calcareous
ch	Chocolate
Cir	Cirripedia
Ck	Chalk
Cl	Clay
Cn	Cinders; Ash
Co	Coral
Co Hd	Coral head
crs	Coarse
dec	Decayed
Di	Diatoms
dk	Dark
fly	Flinty
fne	Fine
Fr	Foraminifera
Fu	Fucus
G	Gravel
Gl	Globigerina
glac	Glacial
gn	Green

Grd	Ground
grd	Ground (Shells)
Grs	Gras
gty	Gritty
gy	Gray
hrd	Hard
K	Kelp
La	Lava
lrg	Large
lt	Light
M	Mud; Muddy
Ma	Mattes
Mds	Madrepores
Ml	Marl
Mn	Manganese
Ms	Mussels
or	Orange
Oys	Oysters
Oz	Ooze
P	Pebbles
Pm	Pumice
Po	Polyzoa
Pt	Pteropods
Qz	Quartz
Rd	Radiolaria
rd	Red
Rk; rky	Rock; Rocky
rt	Rotten
S	Sand
Sc	Scoriae
Sch	Schist
sft	Soft
Sh	Shells
S/M	Surface layer and Under layer
sml	Small
Sn	Shingle
Spg	Sponge
Spi	Spicules
spk	Speckled
St	Stones
stf	Stiff
Stg	Sea-tangle
stk	Sticky
str	Streaky
T	Tufa
ten	Tenacious
unev	Uneven
vard	Varied
vi	Violet
Vol	Volcanic
Vol Ash	Volcanic Ash
Wd	Seaweed
wh	White
yl	Yellow

LIGHT PHASE CHARACTERISTICS

The various light patterns on government aids to navigation are designed not only to help mariners distinguish one aid from another, but also to indicate in darkness what purpose the aid serves.

TABLE XXII. LIGHT PATTERNS OF NAVIGATION AIDS (PRESENT STANDARDS). Chart abbreviations are in parentheses.

Lights that do not change color	Lights that show color variations	Description
Fixed (F)	Alternating (Alt)	A continuous light.
Fixed and flashing (F. Fl.)	Alternating fixed & flashing (Alt. F. Fl.)	Fixed light varied at regular intervals by a more brilliant flash.
Fixed and group flashing (F.Gp.Fl.)	Alternating fixed & group flashing (Alt. F.Gp.Fl.)	Fixed light varied at regular intervals by groups of two or more flashes of greater brilliance.
Flashing (Fl.)	Alternating flashing (Alt. Fl.)	A single flash at regular intervals, not more than 30 per minute, the duration of light being always less than the duration of darkness.
Group flashing (Gp.Fl.)	Alternating group flashing (Alt.Gp.Fl.)	Groups of two or more flashes at regular intervals.
Composite group flashing (Gp.Fl. (1 + 2))		Groups of flashes combined in alternate groups of different numbers.
Morse "A" (Mo.(A))		Short-long flash.
Quick flashing (Qk.Fl.)		Not fewer than 60 flashes per minute.
Interrupted quick flashing (I.Qk.Fl.)		Groups of quick flashes.
Equal interval (E.Int.)		Light on and off for equal intervals.

Continued

Lights that do not change color	Lights that show color variations	Description
Occulting (Occ.)	Alternating occulting (Alt.Occ.)	A light totally eclipsed at intervals, but the period of light always greater than the duration of darkness.
Group occulting (Gp.Occ.)		A light with a group of two or more eclipses at regular intervals.
Composite group occulting (Gp.Occ. (2 + 3))		A light in which the occultations are combined in alternating groups of different numbers.

Generally speaking, the more complex patterns are reserved for major aids to navigation, such as the group flash of three white and one red at Gay Head Light, the entrance to Vineyard Sound. The meanings of the simpler lights, whether on buoys or fixed aids, are outlined in the paragraphs that follow.

I. Inland Waters (Lateral System):
   Red or black buoys. Red or white lights on red buoys, green or white lights on black buoys. For ordinary channel markers, the patterns are flashes at frequencies not greater than 30 times per minute, more often every 2.5, 4, or 6 seconds. At sharp turns or sudden constrictions in the channel, or to mark wrecks or dangerous obstructions, a quick flashing signal — not fewer than 60 flashes per minute — is employed. Also shown on fixed aids.
   Obstruction markers. Horizontally banded red and black buoys, indicating a mid-channel obstruction or a channel junction, always show a pattern (known as "interrupted quick flashing") of quick flashes interrupted by eclipses, repeated six times per minute. Also shown by fixed aids.
   Mid-channel and inlet markers. The black and white vertically banded buoys indicating the middle of the channel or the entrance to an inlet characteristically flash a Morse letter "A" — short-long — with a period of eight seconds.
   Buoys with no directional meaning. Anchorage, fishnet, and dredging buoys use fixed, flashing, or occulting patterns, and their lights may be any color **except** red or green.
II. Western Rivers: Proceeding from seaward, buoys on the port side of the channel employ a flashing pattern. Buoys to starboard utilize group flashes of two. Junction and obstruction buoys use the same interrupted quick-flash pattern as in the Inland system above.

III. Intracoastal Waterway: Entering from north and east and proceeding south and west, light patterns are the same as those of the lateral system.

Figure 7. Light patterns

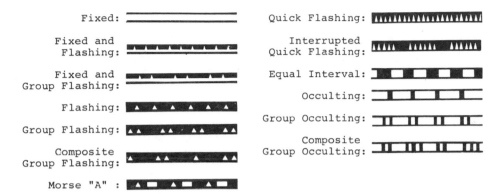

Fixed:		Quick Flashing:	
Fixed and Flashing:		Interrupted Quick Flashing:	
Fixed and Group Flashing:		Equal Interval:	
Flashing:		Occulting:	
Group Flashing:		Group Occulting:	
Composite Group Flashing:		Composite Group Occulting:	
Morse "A" :			

CHART AND PUBLICATION SOURCES

The average chart sales agent authorized to sell the various private and government publications concerned with navigation isn't selling information — he's unloading stock. His selection of charts covering local waters is probably reasonably up-to-date, especially if his is a specialized map store or an outlet in a large marina. But outside his own waters, he could hardly be less concerned. The skipper who wants the best and most reliable material will nearly always benefit by going straight to the publisher, especially when the issuing agency is part of the government and has no profit-motivated interest in disposing of stale stock.

Following are sources of the more important government-issued aids and bulletins that the pilot will want to consider having on board. Many of the books and publications are too unwieldy or specialized for the average ship's library, and many contain much overlapping material. Some, however, are indispensable.

Light List: Published by the Coast Guard in five volumes and available from the Superintendent of Documents, U.S. Government Printing Office, Washington, DC 20402, or chart agents. It is revised annually, so a chart agent's stock is probably the current edition. **Vol. I:** Atlantic Coast from St. Croix River, ME, to Little River, SC; **Vol. II:** Atlantic and Gulf Coasts from Little River, SC, to Rio Grande River, Texas; **Vol. III:** Pacific Coast and islands; **Vol. IV:** Great Lakes; **Vol. V:** Mississippi River.

Local Notice to Mariners: Issued approximately weekly by local Coast Guard districts, these bulletins are available free from the appropriate District Commander. They are not terribly useful unless the new issues are read regularly.

Rules of the Road: May be obtained from the Superintendent of Documents, U.S. Government Printing Office, Washington, DC 20402.

Intracoastal Waterway Booklets: Prepared by the Corps of Engineers, these are comprehensive descriptions of the ICW for the cruising skipper. **Section 1** — Boston to Key West; **Section 2** — Key West to Brownsville, Texas. From Superintendent of Documents, address above.

Coast Pilots: Uncle Sam's own cruising guide, aimed at commercial vessels. Volumes are published annually and are certainly recommended reading for the long-distance cruising man. Available from local chart agents or National Ocean Survey (C44), 6501 Lafayette Ave., Riverdale, MD 20840. Nine volumes: **1** — Eastport, ME, to Cape Cod; **2** — Cape Cod to Sandy Hook; **3** — Sandy Hook to Cape Henry; **4** — Cape Henry to Key West; **5** — Gulf of Mexico, Puerto Rico, Virgin Islands; **6** — Great Lakes; **7** — California, Oregon, Washington, Hawaii; **8** — Alaska (Dixon Entrance to Cape Spencer); **9** — Alaska (Cape Spencer to Beaufort Sea).

Charts: U.S. waters are charted by the NOS (address above), which issues free, updated catalogs in four editions: **1** — Atlantic and Gulf Coasts, including Puerto Rico and the Virgin Islands; **2** — Pacific Coast, including Hawaii, Guam, and Samoa Islands; **3** — Alaska, including the Aleutian Islands; **4** — Great Lakes and adjacent waterways.

Canadian charts are available from: Chart Distribution Office, Department of the Environment, P.O. Box 8080, 1675 Russel Rd., Ottawa, Ontario K1G 3H6.

Charts of foreign waters are published by the Defense Mapping Agency Hydrographic/Topographic Center (DMAHTC) and are available from DMA Office of Distribution Services (DDCP), 6500 Brookes Lane, Washington, DC 20315.

The U.S. Army Corps of Engineers charts the Mississippi River system, and its charts are available as follows:

Lower Mississippi to Ohio River — Vicksburg District, P.O. Box 60, Vicksburg, MI 39180.

Middle and Upper Mississippi and Illinois Waterway to Lake Michigan — Chicago District, 219 S. Dearborn St., Chicago, IL 60604.

Missouri River — Omaha District, 6014 U.S. Post Office and Courthouse, Omaha, NB 68102.

Ohio River — Ohio River Division, P.O. Box 1159, Cincinnati, OH 45201.

List of Lights and **Sailing Directions** for foreign waters are published by the DMAHTC, address opposite. These publications correspond to the **Light List** and **Coast Pilot** for U.S. waters. The Canadian Department of the Environment publishes its own **Sailing Directions** and **List of Lights** for the Great Lakes and Canadian coastal waters.

Tide Tables: Although now generally available in privately published cruising guides, tide tables are available (one volume each for the East Coast, North and South America, and the West Coast, North and South America) from the NOS, address opposite.

Tidal Current Tables: The same information applies as for **Tide Tables.** Two volumes are available, from the NOS.

Tidal Current Charts: Booklets of 12 charts, which follow the ebb and flood of tidal current through each hour of a cycle. These may be used for any year in conjunction with **Tidal Current Tables** (each set of charts is referenced to one primary current station). Coverage is: Boston Harbor; Narragansett Bay to Nantucket Sound; Block Island Sound and Eastern Long Island Sound; Long Island Sound and Block Island Sound; Delaware Bay and River; Upper Chesapeake Bay; Charleston Harbor, SC; San Francisco Bay; Puget Sound, Northern Part; Puget Sound, Southern Part; Tampa Bay. The **Tidal Current Charts** for New York Harbor and for Narragansett Bay (another older chart) must be mentioned separately, since they are referenced to the **Tide Tables.** All are available from the NOS.

Chart books: With the abrupt rise in chart prices over the last decade, private publishers have begun issuing photographic reproductions of NOS charts in full-color, book form. In most cases the charts are slightly reduced from the original size, but seldom enough to make any practical difference in use; the printing and color work are generally excellent. The main attraction of these books is their price — in most cases one can obtain a set of large- and medium-scale charts providing comprehensive coverage of a given area at one-fourth to one-fifth the price of individual government charts.

Chart scales and types: Government charts come in several standard scales and a number of odd ones. Sizes are not standardized, except in the chart booklets intended for small and recreational craft. Small-craft charts consist of several accordion-folded sheets. Information on (but not, annoyingly, the names of) facilities is included. The scale is 1:40,000, with larger-scale insets of harbors. Recreation-craft charts are books of two dozen or more charts, in various scales, covering areas in the Great Lakes only. Harbor charts are printed in scales generally larger than 1:50,000; Coast charts are generally 1:80,000 but may range between 1:50,000 and 1:150,000. General charts, for use offshore at the limits of visibility of navigation aids, are scaled from 1:150,000 to 1:600,000.

LIST OF CHARTS ABOARD

Chart #	Area Covered	Scale	Date

PLOTTING AND LABELING

It's a truism to say that marks on a chart have no meaning until they are labeled, but labeling itself is a form of shorthand, and the average amateur pilot doesn't plot courses frequently enough to develop a consistent system for labeling his courses, lines of position, fixes, etc.

For those whose piloting is of the weekend variety, there is appended here a brief reminder-summary of the standard plotting labels. There is nothing sacred about them, but they do have one salient advantage — being standard, they will be recognized by most seamen, whereas a private system must be explained to each new crewmember.

Courses: Drawn as straight lines from one point to the next. The direction of the course goes above the line, the boat speed through the water goes below. By convention, a plotted course is degrees true if not otherwise specified, and three digits are always used. Additionally, speed is assumed to be knots, unless something else is noted. For most small-craft pilots, true directions are tedious nonsense. Magnetic (**M**) or Compass (**C**) headings will often be simpler and more effective. Add a new label for each course or speed change.

Course line

Lines of Position: Normally, a line of position (LOP) is extended far enough to indicate how the position was obtained — bearing, range, or otherwise. There is, however, no need to run lines clear across the chart.

For a range, above the line note time to the nearest minute, using the 24-hour system. There is no label below the line, which intersects the two or more items used in establishing the range.

For a bearing, note time above the line, true bearing below. (Again, if you use a magnetic bearing, label accordingly.) A bearing advanced has the first time and the time advanced above the line, the bearing below.

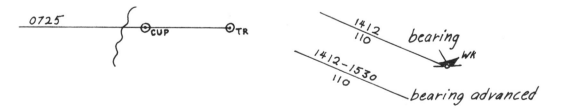

Circle of Position: Put in enough of the arc with a compass to indicate that it is a circle. Note time above, distance off to the nearest tenth of a mile below.

Horizontal Angle: Between the intersecting lines forming the angle, note its value, including a degree symbol.

Fixes: There are several types of fixes, of varying degrees of accuracy. In plotting a fix, the sources of information involved should be noted in the label, so that you may later assess its accuracy. Whereas labels for lines of position are plotted along the lines they describe, labels for fixes and other points should be plotted in angular contrast to any lines. A fix is indicated as a small open circle, the center of which falls at the best estimate of your location. The label consists of the time (to the nearest minute) and nature of the fix. There are three main types:

1. Fix — a straightforward intersection of two or more lines of position observed more or less simultaneously.

2. Running Fix (R Fix) — two lines of position, taken at significantly different times, with one line advanced to its estimated position at the time of the second LOP.

3. Radio Fix (Rad Fix) — though not often noted as a separate type of positioning, the errors inherent in fixes based on radio bearings are such that a position derived wholly or in part from RDF bearings probably ought to be labeled as such, and considered less reliable than a running fix.

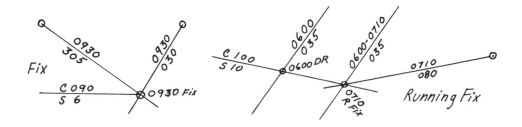

DR: A position derived from dead (or deduced) reckoning (estimating the distance run through the water, according to speedometer or calculation, along the course steered). By definition, a DR plot does **not** take current into consideration. For best accuracy, a DR position should be plotted: (1) at least every time the helmsman is relieved, (2) at every course change, (3) at every speed change, (4) whenever an LOP is obtained. The label is simply the time and the letters **DR.**

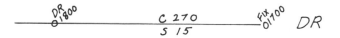

EP: The estimated position is the best possible estimate of true position short of a fix. Usually, this estimate includes not only the effects of current but also any sound estimate of leeway from other causes, speedometer error, steering error, and the like. The appropriate symbol is a small square centered on the position, labeled with the time and the letters **EP.**

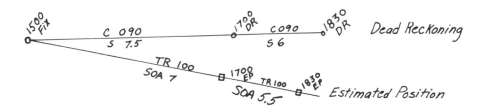

In the diagram above, a boat sailing close-hauled to the eastward is set down by a northeast wind. As the amount of leeway is an estimate, the course line taking it into account is labeled **TR,** for intended track, and **SOA,** for speed of advance. If both speed and leeway were known precisely, the line to the EP would be labeled **COG** (course over the ground) above and **SOG** (speed over the ground) below.

SOLVING THE CURRENT VECTOR DIAGRAM

As a general rule, the skipper has a good idea of the course he is steering, an adequate notion of his boat's speed through the water, and an estimate of the set (direction) and drift (velocity) of the current. In this situation, the navigator first lays off his DR track (the course without regard to current) on the chart. Using his boat's speed, he then demarcates a convenient segment (usually equivalent to a one-hour advance) either along the plotted course or on a separate piece of paper, as shown. The resultant DR position is where the boat should be, current aside, at the end of an hour's run.

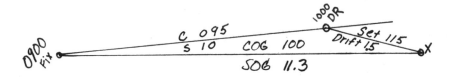

Next he plots — using the dead-reckoned position as a starting point — a line in the direction of the current's set and proportional in length to its drift, using the same units of length as for the DR plot. For convenience, let's label the end of this line **X.** By connecting **X** to the point of origin of the one-hour DR segment, the skipper obtains a line, the direction and length of which represent the intended track and speed. The point, **X,** now becomes the skipper's EP after a one-hour run. The length of the intended track can simply be scaled up or down for runs of durations longer or shorter than one hour. Tidal currents, of course, change with respect to drift (and sometimes set) throughout their cycle.

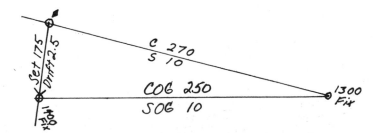

When the boat sails a known course at a known speed and arrives at an unexpected destination, an unknown current is probably the cause. In this case, the navigator plots the DR position and the actual position, then solves for set and drift by connecting the two points, as below. Now he has a known set and drift to work with for the next leg of the voyage, and he can allow for them in advance.

7/ COMMUNICATIONS

Nearly all coastwise cruising yachts today carry some form of radio communications gear as a matter of course, although many skippers have only the foggiest notion of how to use a two-way radio. On a small cruising sailboat with a masthead antenna, a 25-watt VHF/FM transceiver (transmitter-receiver) has a boat-to-boat range of approximately 25 miles. Because U.S. Coast Guard stations, which monitor FM Channel 16, have very high antennas, one can expect 40- to 50-mile ranges when speaking with the USCG.

Coastal pilots generally carry VHF/FM sets by choice. If they go offshore frequently, they may also employ single sideband (SSB) or ham transmitters. For local cruising, some vessels carry Citizens Band equipment, although both reception and transmission are spotty, even over open water. The Coast Guard monitors CB Channel 9, but without enthusiasm. A vessel that is used for serious cruising should undoubtedly carry an emergency position-indicating radiobeacon (EPIRB), as well as a two-way radio. An EPIRB is an automatic transmitter, activated by a switch or by immersion, that broadcasts a single note on the civilian and military aircraft emergency frequencies, presumably monitored by all commercial and military aircraft. If activated in coastal waters, an EPIRB should bring a response quite quickly, as specially equipped Coast Guard ships and planes can home on the signal. One note: many skippers who trigger their EPIRBs make the mistake of turning them off after a few minutes' operation, to conserve the battery. This is a major mistake, as it takes time to be heard and time for Coast Guard direction finders to work. Once the set is on, leave it on.

Although flag signaling is generally obsolete, many commercial vessels fly single-flag signals that can be important to yachtsmen, and of course many of the International Code flags are used as racing signals. Flashing-light Morse code signals are generally only seen when a commercial vessel is trying to attract the attention of a small craft that is not answering radio signals. Still, this mode of communication can be useful, too, if other methods fail, and it's necessary to be able to pick out two- or three-letter Morse code identifiers transmitted by radiobeacons.

VHF/FM CHANNELS AND USAGE

Marine radiotelephones in the VHF/FM band may have something like 50 channels installed, not counting the three receive-only channels for NOAA weather forecasts (see Chapter One). Many of these channels are, however, of little use to the recreational boat operator, and some are forbidden to him. In selecting a marine transceiver, the yachtsman can choose from a broad spectrum of types, from the hand-held portable units — with one to three watts of transmitter power and no more than six possible channels — to transistorized sets with all the channels, usable or not.

The paragraphs that follow catalog, rather like a Chinese restaurant menu, the channels available for different purposes. Figuring out what you'll need in your transceiver is a matter of picking one channel from group A, two from group B, and so on. Before choosing ship-to-ship or marine operator channels, however, it's a good idea to check your boating area and determine what other people have in their sets, and what frequencies the local marine operators use.

A. Emergency and calling

Channel 16 is the internationally recognized distress frequency, the one on which you should initiate a "Mayday" call (described in this chapter). Normal ship's-business calls are begun on Channel 16 and then shifted to a working frequency unless you are calling the marine telephone operator (see below), **or** you have prearranged to call someone on a working frequency without initiating matters on Channel 16. You are required by the FCC to carry Channel 16 in your transceiver. Furthermore, if your VHF/FM radio is turned on, and you are not transmitting or receiving communications, you are required to monitor Channel 16.

B. Intership safety

Channel 6 is a ship-to-ship frequency, restricted to safety communication. It can also be used to talk with the Coast Guard during search-and-rescue operations, but you should not use it (as many do) for a ship-to-ship business frequency. You are required to have Channel 6 in your set.

C. U.S. Coast Guard

Channel 22 is set aside specifically for communication with the vessels and shore stations of the Coast Guard, although they do not regularly monitor this frequency. Establish contact first on Channel 16, then request permission to switch to 22, which Coast Guard personnel sometimes refer to as "22 Alfa."

D. Navigation

Channel 13 is restricted to safety communications between ships, pertaining to maneuvering or directing the vessels' movements. It may also be used for communication between ships and some coastal stations, notably bridges that can be opened. Although any vessel may use Channel 13, it is almost exclusively employed by commercial craft. One-watt transmitting power is the maximum allowed.

E. Port Operations

Channels 5, 12, 14, 20, 65, 66, 73, 74, and 77 are used for messages concerning the operational handling, movement, and safety of vessels in or near ports, locks, and waterways. Note: Channel 77 is restricted to commercial pilots and Channels 11, 12, 13, and 14 are used for vessel traffic service on the Great Lakes, St. Lawrence Seaway, and designated major ports.

F. Noncommercial Operations

Channels 9, 68, 69, 70, 71, 72, and 78 (also known as 78A) are the primary ship-to-ship channels for pleasure craft. You may initiate calls on any of these channels. These frequencies, except for Channels 70 and 72, may also be used for ship-to-shore service. Commercial vessels and many marinas use Channel 9.

G. Commercial Operations

Channels 7, 8, 9, 10, 11, 18, 19, 67, 79, 80, and 88 are primarily used by commercial interests, either ship-to-ship or ship-to-coast. Channel 9 is shared with pleasure craft, Channel 11 is used for port operations (see above), Channels 8, 67, and 88 may not be used for ship-to-shore communication. Pleasure craft are not allowed to use these channels (except for 9). Channel 88 is not available on the Great Lakes or St. Lawrence Seaway.

H. Marine Operator

Channels 24, 25, 26, 27, 28, 84, 85, 86, 87, and 88 are employed in the marine ship-to-shore service. Two or more channels are generally assigned to shore stations in a given boating area. Check with other skippers or the technician who services your set for the numbers of the appropriate area frequencies. The entire call may be conducted on the marine operator frequency, but if you are in an area where you don't know the marine operator's channel, you may simply call the marine operator on Channel 16, and then switch.

I. State Control

Channel 17 is restricted to state and local government.

J. Environmental

Channel 15 is a receive-only frequency reserved for the broadcast by government authority of weather, sea conditions, time signals, notices to mariners, and the like. It is seldom used.

K. Weather

Channels WX1, WX2, and WX3 provide continuous NOAA weather information. See Chapter One for locations of transmitters.

L. U.S. Government

Channels 21, 23, 81, 82, and 83 are restricted to government use. Civilian craft may not use them, except when specifically authorized (the Coast Guard Auxiliary on official business uses Channel 83).

Radiotelephone usage

The Federal Communications Commission has established a number of regulations governing use of the marine radiotelephone. Because of the large number of users and the confusion about and lack of interest in the regulations, there is general ignorance of the details of usage of this marine service. Following are some of the more important regulations as well as some tips for more efficient use of your set.

When making an ordinary ship's-business call, listen before transmitting, to make sure the channel is clear. Your call should consist first of the name of the boat you're calling (repeated if they are not expecting your call or if the airwaves are crowded), then your own boat's name and call sign: "John B, John B, John B, this is Sporadic, WFX 2230." You may call for 30 seconds, but if the person you are calling does not answer, you must wait two minutes before calling the same station again. When you make contact with the other vessel, switch immediately to a ship-to-ship working frequency. Try to plan your calls in advance, so you can place the call on a working frequency and avoid Channel 16 entirely. At the end of the communication, repeat your vessel's name and call sign and say "Out," which means that the message is finished and no reply is expected. "Over," on the other hand, means, "I have finished transmitting a statement or question and await your reply." "Over and out" is incorrect.

Pan is the urgency signal, to be used when the safety of a person or vessel is in jeopardy, but not in instant danger — when, for instance, the engine has broken down and the vessel is drifting toward shore. Use the word **Pan** twice, then send the urgency message.

Security — pronounced "Saycuritay" — is the safety signal, used to alert all stations that a subsequent message concerns navigational safety — a floating obstruction in a channel, for instance. These messages are usually initiated by the Coast Guard.

Always keep transmissions as brief and succinct as possible, but do not use CB or radio jargon if it is likely to confuse an unaccustomed listener.

Get off or stay off the air when an emergency ("Mayday"), urgency, or navigational safety message is broadcast.

Most microphones of the push-to-talk variety work best when you speak in a normally loud voice with the unit about an inch from your lips. Speak slowly and distinctly, especially if transmission is difficult.

General calls, such as "any vessel for a radio check," are prohibited by the FCC. Wait until you can identify a vessel that has just finished a communication, and call him.

In case of emergency, be prepared to spell your boat's name and the names of the crew phonetically; fill in emergency data in advance on the inside back cover of this book.

The Coast Guard and some other rescue agencies can home on your VHF/FM transmission. If you have to abandon a sinking vessel, and you have been in touch with the Coast Guard, leave the radio on and tape down the microphone transmit switch as you go.

IN AN EMERGENCY (see inside back cover)

If you are threatened by grave and imminent danger, transmit the International Distress Call — "MAYDAY, MAYDAY, MAYDAY. THIS IS (name of vessel and call number, repeated three times, slowly and clearly)." Use either 2182 kHz or 156.8 MHz (Channel 16).

If you require assistance or information from the Coast Guard, but are not in distress, call the Coast Guard on either of the above frequencies.

What an assisting vessel needs to know:
1. Your boat's name and call letters.

2. Your location — preferably true bearing in nautical miles from a prominent geographical point. (Use charted name, not local term.)
3. What is wrong.
4. Number and condition of persons aboard.
5. Kind of assistance required.
6. Present seaworthiness of your vessel.
7. Description of your boat: length, type, cabin, masts, power, color of hull, superstructure, trim.
8. Frequencies on your radiotelephone.

If you see another boat in trouble:

Before calling the Coast Guard, make sure you have as much of the following information as possible.
1. Your position and that of distressed vessel.
2. Nature of distress or difficulty.
3. Accurate description (see above) of vessel in distress.
4. Your vessel's capabilities and intentions.
5. Your vessel's name, call letters, available frequencies.

Aircraft distress procedure:

The international signal for an aircraft that wants to direct a ship or boat to a distress is made by circling the vessel and opening and closing the throttle or changing propeller pitch while passing ahead of the surface vessel; aircraft will then fly toward the distress, and surface craft should follow. If assistance is no longer required, aircraft will cross your wake, opening and closing throttle. Surface craft should attempt to make contact with aircraft on either of two international calling frequencies above, and be alert for dropped message container.

Emergency equipment aboard:

	Location	Date Checked
Flares	_____	_____
Extinguishers	_____	_____
First-aid kit	_____	_____
Water lights	_____	_____
Raft	_____	_____
Water/food	_____	_____

KEEPING A RADIO LOG

If your pleasure boat is equipped with a marine band or VHF/FM transmitter, you are required to keep a radio log. The only entries that must be made in the log for a voluntarily equipped station are as follows:

1. Each page must show the vessel name and call sign;
2. Each entry must be signed by the person making that entry;
3. All distress calls heard or transmitted must be logged;
4. All urgent ("Pan") and safety ("Security") communications transmitted must be logged;
5. All transmitted information related to marine safety must be logged;
6. Any installation, maintenance, and repair work must be logged and signed by the licensed technician doing the work.

Logs must be retained one year after date of last entry, and must be shown on request to an authorized FCC representative. Logs containing entries relating to distress traffic must be kept for three years.

If a listening watch on the International Distress Frequency is maintained, you must log the times the watch begins and ends — but a formal watch is not required on pleasure craft.

Note: Additional blank log pages are included in Appendix B.

Vessel Name _____   Call Letters _____

Date	Time	Message	Operator

INTERNATIONAL CODE FLAGS AND THEIR MEANINGS

Below are the flags of the International Code, with their single-letter significance, their phonetic rendering, their meaning as a single-flag signal, and their Morse equivalent. Meanings authorized by the U.S. Yacht Racing Union for use by a Race Committee are in bold-face type.

Figure 8. International Code flags

ALFA
. —
I have a diver down; keep clear.

GOLF
— — .

I require a pilot; or, when flown by a fishing vessel: I am hauling nets.

BRAVO
— . . .
I am carrying, loading or discharging dangerous goods.

HOTEL
. . . .

I have a pilot on board.

CHARLIE
— . — .
Affirmative.

INDIA
. .

I am altering my course to port.
Round the ends start rule.

DELTA
— . .
Keep clear of me: I am maneuvering with difficulty.

JULIET
. — — —

I am on fire with dangerous cargo aboard. Keep clear of me.

ECHO
.
I am altering course to starboard.

KILO
— . —

I wish to communicate with you.

FOXTROT
. . — .
I am disabled; communicate with me.

LIMA
. — . .
You should stop your vessel instantly.
Come within hail or follow me.

MIKE

— —

My vessel is stopped and making no way. **Mark signal.**

NOVEMBER

— ·

Negative. **Abandonment signal.**

OSCAR

— — —

Man overboard.

PAPA

· — — ·

Vessel preparing for sea; or, my nets are fast on an obstruction.

QUEBEC

— — · —

My vessel is healthy and I request free pratique.

ROMEO

· — ·

(no significance)

SIERRA

· · ·

My engines are going astern. **Shorten course signal.**

TANGO

—

Keep clear: I am pair trawling. **Club launch: transportation.**

UNIFORM

· · —

You are running into danger.

VICTOR

· · · —

I require assistance.

WHISKEY

· — —

I require medical assistance.

X-RAY

— · · —

Stop carrying out your intentions and watch for my signals. **Individual recall.**

YANKEE

— · — —

I am dragging my anchor. **Life jacket signal.**

ZULU

— — · ·

I require a tug; or, I am shooting nets.

Continued

The International Code flags are so designed that with one exception (Hotel and Kilo) no two flags have the same light-and-dark pattern, thus identification does not necessarily depend on color. (Hotel is white and red; Kilo is yellow and blue. Had the colors in either been reversed, there would be no exceptions.)

NUMERAL PENDANTS

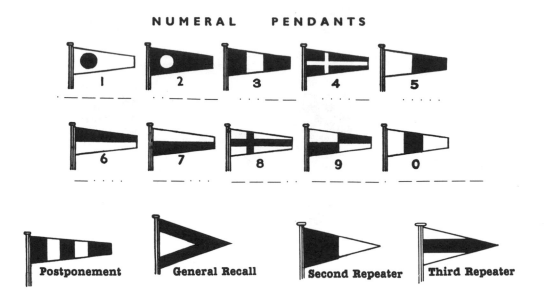

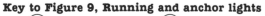

RUNNING LIGHT RECOGNITION

Identifying other vessels' running lights, and reading their message, can be one of the yachtsman's more onerous tasks, for three reasons: first, he simply lacks the necessary accumulated experience to identify easily the many possible patterns; second, even when a vessel is showing the proper lights, there may be visual interference from working lights on her upper decks or from shore lights; third, all too many craft — and especially racing sailboats — display incorrect lights.

What follows is intended as a quick-reference reminder for the crew on watch at night, and a practice guide for the deckhand just learning light patterns. It progresses from the simplest to the more complex, but still reasonably common, combinations. The standard followed here is the International Rules of the Road, since most vessels conform to this scheme. Peculiar or highly unusual patterns — as on anchored dredges and the like — are not included because they generally resemble Christmas trees, and vessels are well advised to stand clear. Bear in mind that running lights on commercial craft may be obscured, as previously mentioned, by other lights aboard, so look carefully before deciding on a large vessel's orientation relative to your own.

Key to Figure 9, Running and anchor lights

(W) = white   (R) = red

(G) = green   (Y) = yellow

Figure 9. Running and anchor lights

LIGHT OBSERVED	SIGNIFICANCE
(W)	Stern light, vessel of any size heading away from observer. 32-point (all-around) anchor light, any vessel under 50 meters long.
(G)	Starboard-side light of a sailboat; if ahead of observer, she is moving from port to starboard of observer's boat.
(R)	Port-side light of sailboat; if danger of collision exists, she probably has the right of way over the observer's boat.

Note: a single red or green light may also be the side light of a vessel being towed. See light patterns for towed craft, below, for associated towboat lights.

LIGHT OBSERVED	SIGNIFICANCE
(G) (R) or (G)(R)	Sailing craft coming directly at the observer. Lights may be separate or a combination of red-green; may be at deck or masthead level.
(W) (W) or (G) (R)	Starboard (far left) or port-side view of engine-powered craft under 50 meters (160 feet) long. May be any type of unspecialized vessel, including sailing yacht using both auxiliary engine and sail.
(W) (G) (R)	Engine-powered vessel less than 50 meters long approaching observer head-on.
(W) (W) (G) (R)	Engine-powered vessel, over 50 meters, heading toward observer. "Masthead" 20-point light forward; a higher, all-around light aft.

99

Ⓦ
 Ⓦ

Ⓖ Ⓡ

Engine-powered vessel approaching observer, but not directly. Two white lights form a range, in this case indicating that the observed vessel is moving from starboard to port relative to observer. Danger exists as long as both red and green are visible.

Ⓦ

  Ⓦ

Ⓖ

Engine-powered vessel, over 50 meters, showing observer her starboard side. No danger of collision should exist.

Ⓡ

Ⓡ

Two vertical red lights in line signify a vessel not under command. In this case, the absence of other lights means she is neither anchored nor aground, and hence may possibly be dangerous to the observer.

Ⓡ

Ⓡ

 Ⓖ

Ⓡ

Ⓡ

 Ⓦ

Ⓦ

Starboard-side view of vessel not under command, yet underway. She displays side lights but no range lights. A vessel aground shows two vertical red lights plus proper anchor lights for a craft of her size — one white, all-around light forward, or, if she is over 50 meters in length, two such lights, one forward and one aft. Although not required, she will probably also have various deck and working lights visible.

Ⓦ

Ⓡ

 Ⓖ

Ⓦ

Ⓡ

Ⓦ

Pilot vessels show white-over-red all-around lights on a signal mast, in addition to the proper running or anchor lights for a powered vessel of their size. Upper illustration is the starboard side of a pilot boat underway. Lower sketch is a pilot vessel proceeding directly away from the observer.

Ⓖ

Ⓦ

 Ⓖ

Green-over-white all-around lights (plus appropriate running lights) are the identifier for a vessel trawling. This is the starboard side of such a vessel.

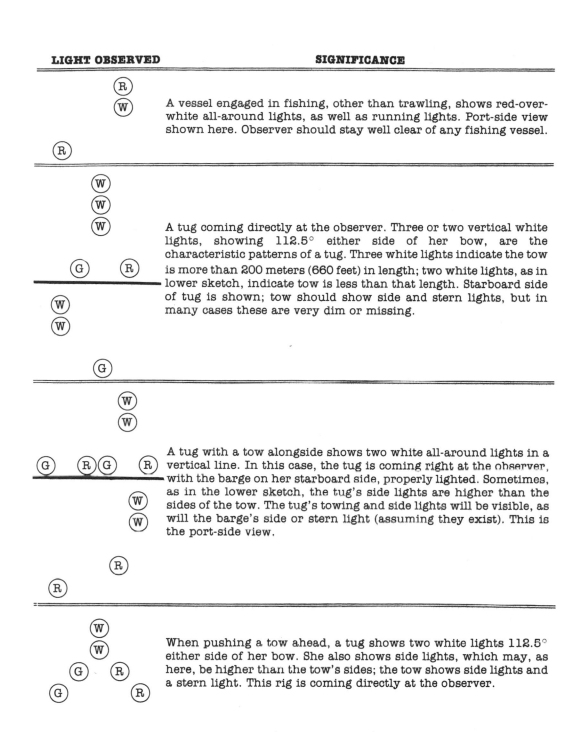

A vessel engaged in fishing, other than trawling, shows red-over-white all-around lights, as well as running lights. Port-side view shown here. Observer should stay well clear of any fishing vessel.

A tug coming directly at the observer. Three or two vertical white lights, showing 112.5° either side of her bow, are the characteristic patterns of a tug. Three white lights indicate the tow is more than 200 meters (660 feet) in length; two white lights, as in lower sketch, indicate tow is less than that length. Starboard side of tug is shown; tow should show side and stern lights, but in many cases these are very dim or missing.

A tug with a tow alongside shows two white all-around lights in a vertical line. In this case, the tug is coming right at the observer, with the barge on her starboard side, properly lighted. Sometimes, as in the lower sketch, the tug's side lights are higher than the sides of the tow. The tug's towing and side lights will be visible, as will the barge's side or stern light (assuming they exist). This is the port-side view.

When pushing a tow ahead, a tug shows two white lights 112.5° either side of her bow. She also shows side lights, which may, as here, be higher than the tow's sides; the tow shows side lights and a stern light. This rig is coming directly at the observer.

Note: On inland waters, a tow pushed ahead should also show, at her bow, a rapidly flashing yellow light.

(Y)
(W)

(W)

A vessel towing astern displays a stern light plus a yellow towing light in line over it. If this combination is visible, the observer should also be able to see another white light — the towed vessel's stern light — below the tug's lights, as shown here. The yellow light is **only** used by towboats.

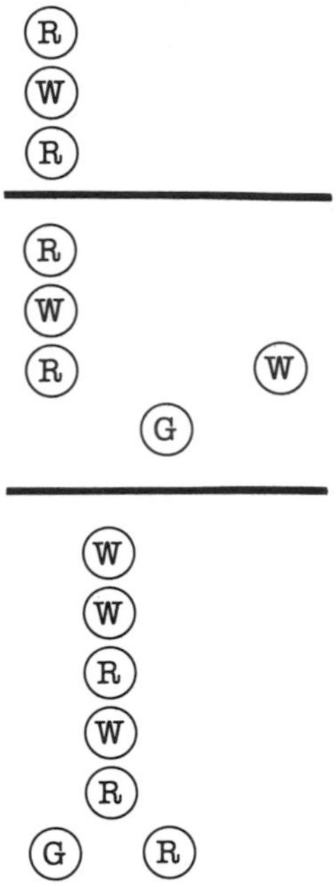

(R)
(W)
(R)

(R)
(W)
(R)   (W)
     (G)

A vessel restricted in her ability to maneuver shows a special identifier — all-around red-white-red in a vertical line — in addition to running lights. The vessel in the upper sketch is not underway, while the one at left is being observed from her starboard side. "Restricted in ability to maneuver" includes vessels engaged in servicing aids to navigation, dredging, surveying, transferring cargo underway, minesweeping, launching or recovering aircraft, or towing — that is, severely restricted in the ability to deviate from course. The bottom sketch shows the very complex light pattern this entails, for a tow less than 200 meters long: two white, 20-point "masthead" lights over the red-white-red vertical all-around pattern, over running lights. This vessel is coming toward the observer, who would do well to get out of the way.

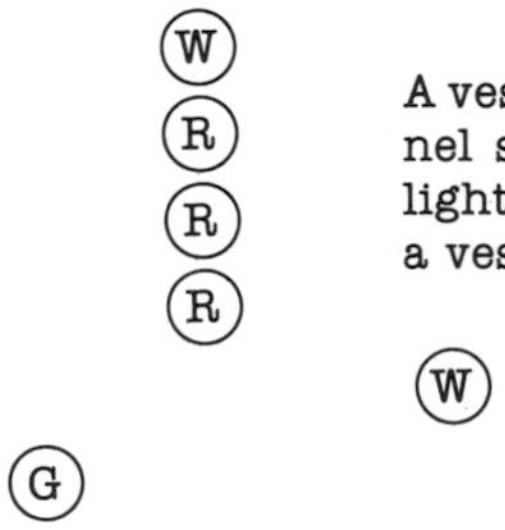

(W)
(W)
(R)
(W)
(R)
(G)   (R)

(W)
(R)
(R)
(R)

(W)

(G)

A vessel constrained by her draft to operate within a dredged channel shows her normal running lights, plus three all-around red lights in vertical alignment. This is the starboard-side view of such a vessel, over 50 meters in length.

DAYMARKS

Under the new Inland Rules of the Road, which are now in force, certain vessels are granted additional rights of way because of an inability to maneuver according to the rules. Ordinary power-driven and sailing craft must give way to these vessels — craft engaged in fishing, restricted in their ability to maneuver, or not under command. At night, each shows a special pattern of lights indicating the condition in question (see previous section). In daylight hours, these vessels display the following special shapes.

Engaged in fishing: two cones in a vertical line with their apexes touching; fishing vessels under 20 meters in length may instead display a basket in the rigging.

Not under command: two balls or similar shapes in a vertical line.

Restricted in ability to maneuver: three shapes in a vertical line — ball, diamond, ball.

Vessel at anchor: a single ball forward.

Vessel with a diver down: either the not-under-command daymark **or** a rigid replica of the International Code flag "A".

Vessel proceeding under both sail and power, if 12 meters or more in length: a conical shape, apex downward. ▼

All shapes are to be shown "where they can best be seen," usually in the rigging forward.

APPENDIX A

FORMULAS FOR THE CALCULATOR

The hand-held calculator has become indispensable for many skippers. While there are all sorts of calculators, from the simplest electronic adding machines to the so-called "dedicated" calculators preprogrammed for navigational functions, perhaps the most common one for navigational purposes is the scientific or slide-rule unit, which has sine, cosine, and tangent keys, their inverses, and log, square, and square root keys, and addressable memory. If the machine is capable of working in units of degrees, minutes, and seconds of arc (or hours, minutes, and seconds of time) and converting them to their decimal equivalents, so much the better. At least one addressable memory is a must. Here are some handy formulas for the calculator. Others will occur to the mariner as he uses the instrument.

Distance to the horizon
$1.144 \sqrt{EYE} = D$ (nautical miles), and
$1.317 \sqrt{EYE} = D$ (statute miles),
where EYE equals the observer's height of eye in feet above water level, and D equals distance.

Vertical sextant angle (base of object visible)
$\frac{H \times .566}{A} = D$, where H is the height of the object in feet, A is the angle,

in minutes and tenths of a minute of arc, subtended between its top and bottom, and D is distance off in nautical miles.

Distance off by relative bow and beam bearing and run between
DR x tan A = D, where DR is distance run between bearings, A is bow bearing, D is distance off in nautical miles.

Distance off at second bearing, with two bow bearings and run between
$$\frac{DR \times \sin A}{\sin (B - A)} = D,$$ where DR is distance run in nautical miles, A is the first bow bearing, B is the second bow bearing, and D is distance off.

Distance traveled to reach a mark dead to windward
$$\frac{200}{\sin \text{ tacking angle}} \times (\sin \text{ angle of attack}) = D,$$ where tacking angle is the number of degrees from close-hauled on one tack to close-hauled on the other, angle of attack is the angle relative to the base course, and D is the ratio of the distance traveled to the straight-line distance, expressed as a percentage.

Example: A yacht that tacks through 90° is headed for a mark 10.5 miles to windward. How far must she sail? $\frac{200}{\sin 90} \times \sin 45 = 141\% = 14.85$ mi.

Distance sailed when tacking downwind
$$\frac{2 \times DL \times \sin A}{\sin (2A)} = D,$$ where DL is straight-line distance downwind to the mark, A is the relative angle of divergence from straight-line course, and D is the distance sailed.

Example: A navigator sailing downwind wants to increase his speed by sailing alternating broad reaches, each one 20° off the base course. If the mark is 15 miles downwind, $\frac{2 \times 15 \times \sin 20}{\sin (2 \times 20)} = 15.96$ mi.

Reduction of draft when a boat is heeled
Heeled draft = (cos of angle of heel) x draft.

Example: A boat that normally draws four feet is heeled to 25°. What does she now draw? cos 25 x 4 = 3.625' = 3'7½''.

Compensating for current
Finding course to steer: $C - \arcsin \left[\frac{D \times \sin(S - C)}{B} \right]$, where C is true course to destination, in degrees, B is boat speed in knots, D is current drift in knots, and S is current set in degrees.

Speed made good: $\frac{\sin(A - S) \times \sin B}{\sin(C - S)}$, where A equals course to steer (from previous formula), and other symbols are the same.

106

Vertical sextant angle (base of object hidden by visible horizon)

...and just in case you were wondering why it's necessary to use Table XVI to determine distance off by vertical angle when the object's base is beneath the horizon, here is the formula from which the table is derived:

$$D = \sqrt{\left(\frac{\tan A}{.000246}\right)^2 + \frac{H}{.74736}} - \frac{\tan A}{.000246}$$

— where D is distance off, A is the subtended angle, corrected for error and dip, and H is the difference between the height of the object and the observer's eye height.

APPENDIX B

HEIGHT OF TIDE AT SUBORDINATE STATION

HEIGHT AT ANY TIME   Place _____

    Time _____ Date _____

Reference Station:	Table 2 Differences	Time	Local Height	Tidal Data Duration h. m.	Range ft.	Time from High/Low h. m.	
time ht.	h. m. ft.						Corr'n factor
High							
Low							Ht. of tide
High							Corr'n factor
Low							Ht. of tide
High							Corr'n factor
Low							Ht. of tide

VELOCITY OF CURRENT AT SUBORDINATE STATION

CURRENT AT ANY TIME   Place _____

    Time _____ Date _____

	Reference Station	Table 2 Differences	Local Current	Interval Slack/Max	Interval Slack/Time	
	Time vel.	h. m. v. r.	time vel.	h. m.	h. m.	Corr'n Factor
Slack						
Max	Ebb/Flood					Current Velocity
Slack						Corr'n Factor
Max	Ebb/Flood					Current Velocity
Slack						Corr'n Factor
Max	Ebb/Flood					Current Velocity

108

HEIGHT OF TIDE AT SUBORDINATE STATION

HEIGHT AT ANY TIME   Place_____

                    Time _____Date_____

Reference Station:	Table 2 Differences	Time	Local Height	Tidal Data Duration h. m.	Range ft.	Time from High/Low h. m.	Corr'n factor
time ht. h. m. ft.							
High							
Low							Ht. of tide
High							Corr'n factor
Low							Ht. of tide
High							Corr'n factor
Low							Ht. of tide

VELOCITY OF CURRENT AT SUBORDINATE STATION

CURRENT AT ANY TIME   Place_____

                    Time_____ Date_____

	Reference Station	Table 2 Differences	Local Current	Interval Slack/Max	Interval Slack/Time	
	Time vel.	h. m. v. r.	time vel.	h. m.	h. m.	Corr'n Factor
Slack						
Max	Ebb/Flood					Current Velocity
Slack						Corr'n Factor
Max	Ebb/Flood					Current Velocity
Slack						Corr'n Factor
Max	Ebb/Flood					Current Velocity

HEIGHT OF TIDE AT SUBORDINATE STATION

HEIGHT AT ANY TIME   Place_____

Time _____Date_____

Reference Station:	Table 2 Differences	Time	Local Height	Tidal Data Duration	Range	Time from High/Low	
time ht.	h. m. ft.			h. m.	ft.	h. m.	Corr'n factor
High							
Low							Ht. of tide
High							Corr'n factor
Low							Ht. of tide
High							Corr'n factor
Low							Ht. of tide

VELOCITY OF CURRENT AT SUBORDINATE STATION

CURRENT AT ANY TIME   Place_____

Time_____ Date_____

	Reference Station	Table 2 Differences	Local Current	Interval Slack/Max	Interval Slack/Time	
	Time vel.	h. m.	v. r.	time vel.	h. m.	h. m.	
Slack							Corr'n Factor
Max							Current Velocity
	Ebb/Flood						
Slack							Corr'n Factor
Max							Current Velocity
	Ebb/Flood						
Slack							Corr'n Factor
Max							Current Velocity
	Ebb/Flood						

110

HEIGHT OF TIDE AT SUBORDINATE STATION

HEIGHT AT ANY TIME   Place _____

                          Time _____ Date _____

Reference Station:	Table 2 Differences	Time	Local Height	Tidal Data Duration	Range	Time from High/Low	
time ht.	h. m. ft.			h. m.	ft.	h. m.	Corr'n factor
High							
Low							Ht. of tide
High							Corr'n factor
Low							Ht. of tide
High							Corr'n factor
Low							Ht. of tide

VELOCITY OF CURRENT AT SUBORDINATE STATION

CURRENT AT ANY TIME   Place _____

                          Time _____ Date _____

	Reference Station	Table 2 Differences	Local Current		Interval Slack/Max	Interval Slack/Time	
	Time vel.	h. m. v. r.	time	vel.	h. m.	h. m.	Corr'n Factor
Slack							
Max	Ebb/Flood						Current Velocity
Slack							Corr'n Factor
Max	Ebb/Flood						Current Velocity
Slack							Corr'n Factor
Max	Ebb/Flood						Current Velocity

Radio Log

Vessel _____ Call Letters _____

Date	Time	Message	Operator

Radio Log

Vessel _____ Call Letters_____

Date	Time	Message	Operator

Radio Log

Vessel _____ Call Letters _____

Date	Time	Message	Operator